The Gringos Guide To

Driving Through
MEXICO
&
CENTRAL
AMERICA

by Derek Dodds

Mexico

ISBN 978-1456535094 & 1456535099

Published by Drive Me Loco.

Dedicated to my two seas,
you have changed my world
and opened my heart
to all possibilities.

Te quiero Marleen.

D.D.

Contents

Introduction

One of so many beautiful places that you will find along the
road less traveled. This one was taken in Costa Rica.

"It takes courage to grow up and turn out to be who you really are."
- E.E. Cummings

Mexico and Central America have been frequent travel destinations of mine for over 35 years. The beauty of the coast and the richness of the culture have drawn me back time and time again. It all started in the mid 80's, I had just graduated from high school and I was working a summer job and my Dad calls me and says, "What ya doing for the summer?" I told him I'd be working all summer to save for a surf trip and he said why wait, let's go now. I replied, "what about my job?" and he said, "just quit!" I quit that day; we packed the boards on the car and my first proper surf trip was born, a three month journey to the tip of Baja surfing uncrowded epic southern swell along the way. I never thought that the best advise I'd ever get from my Dad was to quit a job and go surfing. A few years later a friend calls me up and says lets go surf Costa Rica and I found myself quitting yet another job and surfing my brains out in Costa Rica.

Several years later I would travel from California to Costa Rica by car and surf along the way, this guide was born in those moments and over the next two decades I would do several trips through Mexico, Central America and South America. Asia and Australia we next on my travel list, I lived in Bali on and off for a few years and finally made my way to Australia, surfing from the East to the West and scoring some epic wave in New Zealand on my way back . . . home? If you haven't traveled much and would love a wonderful experience please go to Bali! Next I moved to Europe, living in Spain mainly and surfing Portugal, France, and the UK with frequency. I also ventured to the Azores Islands, Morocco, and the Canaries Islands during my three year Euro feast, surf travel was becoming my life, or least a big portion of it. I moved back to the US and started going south again, traveling to Mainland Mexico every six months for the past decade and surfing from Puerto Escondido to Mazatlan, sprinkling in a few trips to Costa Rica, Brazil, Argentina, and Ecuador.

Want to take a unique surf trip? Go surf the Galapagos Islands, it is magical! Next I had Africa on my sites and stumbled upon Jbay in 2004, hands down one of the best waves on the planet. I've been back to South Africa five times since 2004, surfing from Cape Town to Durban and somehow avoiding all the great white sharks along the Transski coast. There are many other places I have surfed on this planet, Japan, Thailand, India, Cuba, China . . .just to name a few. Keep dreaming my friends and make your dreams reality by living the way you want.

The core of this book is based on thirty-five years of experience driving in Mexico and Central America by personal vehicle—starting with my first trip at age five. Driving to Central America was one of the most fantastic and exciting trips of my life. I currently venture into Latin America by car at least every other month and each trip is as enjoyable as the first.

I have compiled information for this book with the hope that more people can enjoy their travels by vehicle through Mexico and Central America. With your own vehicle you have the freedom to go where you want and to see that which you would otherwise never see. However, in every adventure there exists risks and when you drive your own vehicle you assume additional responsibilities that you wouldn't have traveling by bus or plane. I feel the reward outweighs the risk, and hence this book, and thus I support travel in this spectacular part of the world. The splendorous views of nature and the congeniality of the people in the small villages and on the outer limits of large resort towns are absolutely wondrous. The kindness and generosity of the populace touched my heart in ways that continue to resonate in my interior today. My most treasured experiences took place hundreds of miles away from the popular tourist sites in places that were unreachable by public transportation.

In this guide I have included detailed logistical information for the drive as well as personal experiences that either enriched my adventure or added to the occasional trials and tribulations of travel. Hopefully my personal experiences will give you a more realistic idea of what to expect while traveling through Mexico and Central America. Driving through northern Mexico I experienced my first **special encounter** of the trip and thus here in the introduction I want to share with you a small story that if told separately would represent the opulent generosity and genuine benevolence of the Latin culture.

It was the first week of my adventure into the heart of Latin America and I stopped at the side of the road to concoct my daily caffeine jolt which ritualistically prepared me for the next hundred miles of driving. Woe-fully, the graceless roads had split my one-gallon water bottle in half and I had foolishly placed my matches next to the bottle and thus converted my matches into a soggy mess. Without the matches I couldn't ignite my portable stove, (I pass along the first lesson of this book which is to always store matches in a zip-lock bag or similarly constructed apparatus in order to protect them from accidental spills). I possess a great affinity for coffee, some would even suggest that I have an addiction, and those travelers that have the same weakness for this legal drug know the seriousness of this travesty. Fortunately, the coffee Gods sent a Mexican boy to my rescue. After hearing of my predicament he rapidly peddled his barely operable bicycle toward a far off shack and after several minutes he returned with a lighter and his adorable younger sister. Through a personalized form of sign language, which I have perfected after several years of traveling in countries in which I do not know the language, and the ever so popular Spanglish, which has infiltrated the Western United States and I believe to be the language of the future in the places like California, I conveyed that the lighter was empty, it went something like this, "no...hay...um...agua... um...gas...in...esta...luz." Like a bolt of thunder he was off again toward the house with his sister left behind to keep me company. At first I thought that my idiotic display of dyslexic charades had frightened him into seclu-sion but I later learned that he actually understood my attempt at com-munication and even more surprising was the fact that his entire family seemed to carry a genetic gift that enabled them this remarkable ability at non linguistic communication. Moments later he returned with matches, his father, his uncle, and a neighbor and for the following two hours my new friends and I shared a pot of coffee and talked about Mexico, at least I think we were talking about Mexico? This is an example of the type of experience that you can expect to have while driving through Mexico and Central America. By the way, they gave me a box of matches for my ensu-ing caffeine fix.

You must give serious consideration to the type of vehicle that transports you from point A to point B, wherever that might be. You don't have to drive a 4X4 to be comfortable on your trip. You do need a reliable vehicle that will withstand hard driving. The ideal vehicle for driving comfortably in Central America has the following: **normal to above-normal road clearance, good tires, good shocks, air conditioning, cassette player, tinted windows, gas mileage above 20 m.p.g., fog and road lights, and an attentive driver.** If you spend a little extra money to prep your vehicle before the trip you will thank yourself when you return from your journey. Before my trip I spent about $400 dollars replacing all the fluids, belts, electrical fittings and hoses. Take the used car parts with you on your trip, there are no auto supply warehouses along the way. Throw in an extra fuel filter, a spare tire, your basic mechanical tool assortment, and anything else you feel will assist you with minor repairs. Tires! Tires! Tires! Please, fit your vehicle with a good set of tires. The majority of the roads are horrible and your best defense is a reliable set of tires. If you have some extra money and your shocks are old, my recommendation is to replace them. Shake, Rattle and Roll takes on a new meaning while driving through Mexico and Central America and if your shocks are non-existent before your trip, you can expect your spine to be in a similar condition at the end of your excursion.

In concluding these words of wisdom I would like to wish everyone a successful and safe journey. Preparation is the key to a successful excursion, have a great trip, and remember that the adventure is in the journey and not the final destination!

Carpe Diem.

Derek Dodds
Ojai, California, January 2011
Drivemeloco.com

Chapter
ONE
The Basics

Cortez was a Spanish conquistador who led an expedition that caused the fall of the Aztec Empire and brought large portions of mainland Mexico under the rule of the King of Castile in the early 16th century, I am surprised that many of these statues are still standing.

It is better to live one year in the life of a tiger than 100 years in the life of a sheep.

~ Tibetan Saying

Welcome fellow adventurer! This loco guide offers detailed information, road maps, general driving advice and fun stories about the drive through Mexico and Central America. If you are thinking about driving through Mexico and Central America you must read this travel guide.

For information about hotels consult check wavetribe.com for information around popular surf locations or logon to our official travel site drivemeloco.com for updates and travel products to make your trip more enjoyable.

The city to city portion of this guide is constructed as follows: firstly, the starting location and ending location for each section are printed in bold capital lettering—NOGALES/GUYAMAS; secondly, detailed driving statistics are listed—Driving Time: 6 hours, Kilometers: 421, Miles: 261, Hwy: 15; thirdly, a map is displayed for each particular section with the major cities along the route and the respective highway numbers; lastly, a short description of the drive is given along with a Special Directions and Lessons Learned section.

Study the Special Directions sections for clarification of specific instructions for each detailed area. The Learned Lessons section highlights special areas of concern. Additionally, the Hotel & Eats section provides travelers with specific hotel and restaurant recommendations that I felt deserve special attention. Also note that Spanish words and cities are written in italics for improved readability. The following are examples of the aforementioned:

Special Directions
All the paperwork for personal vehicles and tourist cards are processed at the Immigration/Customs checkpoint 24k after the US-Nogales border entry which is located outside of town. You are not required to process any paperwork at the actual border entry point. Drive directly out of town and follow the signs to Guaymas.

Learned Lessons

When gringos ask for directions in a Latin American country, they will always get a different answer. Thus, ask several people the same question and go with the most popular answer.

For Your Information & Enjoyment

Throughout the guide you will find general information sporadically displayed to inform the reader of various important topics.

The Drive

The drive through Mexico and Central America is a wonderful experience; however, it's not an adventure for everyone. The following pages contain my advice and detailed accounts of my experiences while driving through Mexico and Central America. Places and conditions change, thus be prepared to make variations or detours altered from the original directions; though generally speaking things in Central America change slowly. There is no one correct way of doing anything and therefore if you find a way or route that you feel is easier or less complicated, please send your comments to the address at the end of this book so that your information may be included in the next publication.

Which Route?

There are three routes through Mexico, one is along the Atlantic Coast (actually the Gulf of Mexico), the second is through Central Mexico and Mexico City, and the third is by the way of the Pacific Coast. From Texas the four main entry points are El Paso, Piedras Negras, Laredo and Brownsville. There are several east-west, north-south links as you journey south through Mexico. The Pacific Coast route is the hands down favorite among travelers. The roads are better overall, drivers don't have to circumnavigate Mexico City, and there are plenty of beautiful sites along the way. Those travelers that have driven all three routes agree that the Pacific Coast route is by far the best. The route detailed in the city-by-city portion of this book is the Pacific Coast route.

If Central America is your goal, then the central route bogs you down too much in Mexico City and the surrounding areas. The Atlantic route is just plain hard on vehicles and the scenic delightful places are fewer. My recommendation is to head for the Pacific Coast and then south through Mexico.

Increased road check points are anticipated for the future—Mexico is getting pressure from the US to help stop illegal immigration and sniff out terrorist activity. Most often once officials see your gringo face an unrestrained passage can be expected.

In situations where you are motioned to pull over the officers will ask a few general questions and then check your vehicle or migration paperwork. No problem, always present a polite and respectful attitude and the officers will do the same. Idiotic, disrespectful travelers can expect a synonymous response from officials.

If you are traveling with a fluent Spanish speaker, have that person deal with the officials. All things being equal in these situations, have a woman talk to a man and a man talk to a women when dealing with border officials or customs inspectors.

Important Documents

Carry your auto registration and vehicle ownership papers with you. You must have the title to the car in your possession on the trip, it must be the original and not a copy. A Mexican tourist visa is required and is issued at the border. Additional items you need include your passport, auto insurance papers, Guatemalan visa and photocopies of everything. Visa requirements are constantly changing, thus check with each consulate before you leave. Do yourself a favor and obtain the necessary visas before you depart from the US. This saves a lot of time and confusion when entering countries like Guatemala and Nicaragua. In most instances obtaining visas for all the countries takes only a day or two at the embassies in the US—a little preparation before the trip goes a long way.

A United States driver's license is valid throughout Central America and Mexico—however it is recommended that you get an International Driving Permit. You can get one by filling out a form available from the AAA (http://www.aaa.com/vacation/idpf.html) and returning it with $15.00 and two copies of your passport type photo. If you return your application in person to the AAA office, they will issue it immediately to you. But if you prefer, return the application by mail and it will be mailed to you. The passport photos can easily be obtained from your local photo shop for about $20. The permit is valid for one year.

When you need to present your license to the police or military, show them the international license; see if you can get away with not showing your US state license. If for some reason your license is confiscated, let them take your international license. That will permit you to drive with your US license. This doesn't always work, but it's worth a try. Technically you are required to present both the driving permit and your US state license, but you will rarely be asked for your US license. By the way, don't forget to use the international license when filing out border documents. Be consistent, the police or military may ask for papers during transit and they may notice a discrepancy if you use one for the paperwork and then another for roadside inspections.

Which Vehicle is Best?

You must give serious consideration to the type of vehicle that transports you from point A to point B, wherever that might be. You don't have to drive a 4X4 to be comfortable on your trip. You do need a reliable vehicle that will withstand hard driving. The ideal vehicle for driving comfortably in Central America has the following: normal to above-normal road clearance, good tires, good shocks, air conditioning, CD player and IPod, tinted windows, gas mileage above 20 m.p.g., fog and road lights, and an attentive driver. If you spend a little extra money to prep your vehicle before the trip you will thank yourself when you return from your journey. Before my trip I spent about $400 dollars replacing all the fluids, belts, electrical fittings and hoses.

Take the used car parts with you on your trip—there are no auto supply warehouses along the way. Throw in an extra fuel filter, a spare tire, your basic mechanical tool assortment, and anything else you feel will assist you with minor repairs. Tires! Tires! Tires! Please, fit your vehicle with a good set of tires. The majority of the roads are horrible and your best defense is a reliable set of tires. If you have some extra money and your shocks are old, my recommendation is to replace them. Shake, Rattle and Roll takes on a new meaning while driving through Mexico and Central America and if your shocks are nonexistent before your trip, you can expect your spine to be in a similar condition at the end of your excursion.

Driving Through Cities

Most of the roads in Mexico go directly through cities and towns. Once you are in a city you must find your way through the city and on to your next destination. Find a large truck or bus that is transiting through the city and follow it. Trucks and buses move through the city and on to the highway using the most direct route—thus providing a personal guide out of the city and on to the major highway. Additionally, following large obstructing vehicles through the city provides cover for your gringo...I am a target . . . license plates and essentially the large trucks hide you from plain view. Obstructed, the city policeman, sipping his cold Corona, cannot easily see your vehicle. By the time you pass his perch he rarely notices your smiling gringo face.

What To Expect From The Police & Military

The police that will give you the most problems are the small-time city police. These police are poorly educated, minimally trained and mostly corrupt. They think that as a tourist you owe them compensation for transiting through their minuscule town. If you're pulled over chances are that they will ask you for a small donation. In most cases it is best to play their game and give them something. In Mexico and other Central American countries you are guilty of a crime until proven innocent, not innocent until proven guilty. Nevertheless, you don't want an over ambitious police officer creating some false crime or planting illegal contraband in your vehicle because you wouldn't give him a small bribe.

Often when stopped, the police or military will ask, "Where are you coming from?" (donde viene?). Just tell them the next tourist town—looking like a tourist helps too.

In most Central American countries the police are part of the military, except Costa Rica and Panama. In the larger cities of Honduras traffic police are a common site. In Honduras they wear a gray uniform with a black strip along the side of their legs. In most Central American countries the likelihood of being stopped periodically for inspections is a common occurrence. The officials will ask you for your license and vehicle registration card. Often they will ask for your passport as well. Once they realize you are a tourist they will wave you on through.

The current administration in most Central American countries and in Mexico is trying to put on a good face for tourists; rarely would you expect to have any hassles. There are a variety of reasons for the periodic inspections. The main reason is to remind people that the military is in control, even in these "democratic" countries.

Throughout Central America and Mexico the military presence is a fact of life. North Americans are not accustomed to seeing armed military on a crowded downtown street, but this is a common sight in Central America. The reasons for the periodic military stops range from looking for stolen vehicles to inspecting for contraband, such as arms or drugs. An effort is being made to control the amount of arms in civilian hands—this is one of the major efforts now being made.

The Police

The police that will give you the most problems are the small-time city police. These police are poorly educated, minimally trained and mostly corrupt. They think that as a tourist you owe them compensation for transiting through their minuscule town. If you're pulled over chances are that they will ask you for a small donation. In most cases it is best to play their game and give them something. Remember, in Mexico and other Central American countries you are guilty of a crime until proven innocent, not innocent until proven guilty. Nevertheless, you don't want an over ambitious police officer creating some false crime or planting illegal contraband in your vehicle because you wouldn't give him a small bribe.

Propina, Bribes & Traffic Tickets

For those from the United States, more often than not, an interaction with the police or military is actually an opportunity to give him a donation—less so with the military. Finesse, calm and using your head are the order of the day. Do your best to be pleasant, show him the documentation he needs, don't forget to try and give him the International driving permit and not your state license. (1) Make him aware you are a visitor and are not familiar with the driving customs. Usually you will be given a warning and permitted to leave. (2) If this doesn't happen, ask him if you could pay your infraction on the spot, put a small bill in your passport and hand it to him to check it out a second time. At this point he usually takes the bill, returns your passport and you leave. (3) Lastly, he will write you an infraction ticket, retain your license, and request you to appear in a court to pay your fine. Should this happen and it is your international license that he has, and your visit is short, you might consider continuing on your journey. If the policeman takes your license and you are license-less (sic) and are stopped again, present the citation to the questioning officer. This will serve as your license.

Police in Mexico or Central America will accept bribes as a means of payment for infractions and other various violations of the law. To put it straight, the official usually wants a small donation. If you break the law, your best solution to an infraction is to pay the fine at the location of the infraction. Tell the officer that you want to pay the fine and ask the officer if he will deliver it to the main station. I have been driving in Mexico for over 35 years and I have been pulled over dozens of times.

There were several instances where I he refused to pay the fine on the spot and thus went through the bureaucratic process of paying the fine at the station. Paying the fine at the station entails hours of paperwork and always equates to a much larger payment than what would have been paid to the officer at the location. Thus, negotiate the smallest sum possible and pay the officer on location.

Crime

In everything good there is also something bad and therefore I wanted to say a word on crime because this is such a huge topic when traveling into Mexico and Central America. My opinion (and experience) is that there is less crime in Mexico and Central America than in North America, which is also statistically proven. However, travelers are popular targets because they stand out and usually have something worth stealing. Thus the odds substantially increase because you, most likely, are a more desirable target to the criminal than the local farmer that earns in a year what you earn in a month.

The best thing to remember is to use common sense and avoid putting yourself or your valuables in a situation that would invite crime. Most crimes in Mexico and Central America are victimless, but unfortunately not all. Victimless means that Señor Criminal will attempt to take your belongings without physically threatening or harming you. They usually break into your car or hotel room when you are not around. Hence, park in safe places, stay in hotels that have locks on the doors and windows and think defensively when in large cities, (i.e. don't carry your wallet in your back pocket).

In over five months of travel throughout Mexico and Central America in my vehicle I encountered two criminal acts. Unfortunately, the main criminals got away with the crime. While in Dominical, Costa Rica, my car was broken into. My tool box and automotive tools, hiking boots and an empty backpack were taken. While having breakfast the next morning at a local cafe I overheard that the police caught a thief that had broken into several vehicles the night before. I went to the police station and after waiting several minutes to see the sergeant I was told that they had recovered my tools—what actually ended up being about one-third of his tools. After filing a police report and 20 minutes of interrogation by the police . . . wait, I'm the victim remember . . . I received my tools. The next day I noticed that my hiking boots were missing so I returned to the police station to ask if they had retrieved them. To my surprise I found the sergeant in the front of the police station working on the police vehicle with the remainder of my stolen tools. The officer denied that they were mine and he threatened to take my driving permit away if I pressed the issue further. Unfortunately many thieves in Central America ware official uniforms.

Please don't let crime rule your thoughts because most people in Central America are trustworthy, but then again, you must remember that these countries are very poor and that when given an opportunity thieves will take your possessions.

Carrying Arms

There are many people who may consider carrying a pistol for protection. Don't do it! Primarily, if you are caught with a weapon you will not only lose the weapon, but it can very well make your life miserable for some time. Secondarily, your small pistol will be of no assistance against numerous automatic weapons. You would be far out gunned unless you decide to take some type of high powered assault rifle— but I don't recommend it.

Throughout the journey your vehicle will be inspected and some inspections are meticulous. There is a high probability that the weapon will be found. Regardless of what is said here there are travelers that will insist on taking a weapon. If you must take a weapon, carry it on your person and not hidden somewhere in the vehicle, it is very unlikely that any officials will ever search you personally.

I did carry a rather large multipurpose Rambo-looking hunting knife on my trip. I placed it on the dashboard of my vehicle within reaching distance and within plain view. Never did any official comment about the weapon. Though I never used it, just having something made me feel more comfortable while traveling alone through the big cities.

Games Border Officials Like To Play

When you cross from one country into another there are a number of scams that the border officials like to use to get some of your money. Here are samples of a few of them.

The Bring Them In Here Game; Game #1:

Your car must be inspected before you will be permitted to enter the country. The border official will tell you to take everything out of your car and bring it inside the inspection building. After the inspection you will be permitted to take your personal items back to your vehicle and re-pack them again. It is true that your vehicle needs to be inspected, but this can be done at your vehicle. It is unnecessary to take everything out and bring it to the inspection station. Belize, Guatemala and Mexico are especially good at this scam. In Guatemala there are a number of men at the border that earn a living carrying your possessions into the inspection building. Almost always you can negotiate with the inspector (usually the one assisting you with the papers) to have the car inspected with everything intact, but you will need to pay these "gentlemen" for their loss of work. About $5 US each will do it—most often there are four or five to be paid. If you don't have many personal effects, carry them in and you will see that the inspector will hardly look at them, he will just say okay, and you carry them back.

The You Need A List Of Items Game; Game #2:

Your possessions may cause you problems after you enter the country. The officials at the border will tell you that other officials (like the military or town police) may think that you brought your things in illegally. They will suggest that they make a list of everything you brought and that this special list will give you clear passage. The charge for this official looking document ranges from $50 to $100. I thought I would avoid this problem by typing a list of all my possessions before the trip and then showing it to the border officials when they attempted to pull this one on me. The officials liked the list, stamped it with an official looking stamp and charged me a fee anyway. However, the charge was only a few dollars. For the most part, once you have entered into the country, if you are stopped by the police or the military they could care less if you have an official looking document. If their intent is to get a bribe, that document will prove worthless.

The Document Copy Game; Game #3:

You must have copies of all your documents. Officials will claim they must have copies of your car's ownership papers, or other documents. The official will tell you that the copy machine is broken or the official who operates the machine is on vacation, usually in the next room. The official will then tell you that you must pay extra to be allowed to enter. This scheme can easily be avoided by making extra copies of everything before you leave. Have at least on set for each border exit and entry stashed away just for this purpose. Of course it's a scam, but what can you do.

The Oh No You Have A Bug On Your Shoe Game; Game #4:

Your car and perhaps you must be sprayed for insects. There is a small fee for this. Most often, just pay the fee, get sprayed and go on. Many people pay bribes to avoid this, the bribes are often more than the spraying fee. Hopefully a little insecticide won't ruin your day, just leave the windows down for awhile.

Gifts & Bribes

Take used clothing and other miscellaneous items and give them away as you go. These items may also satisfy the police, border guards or military when you meet with the unavoidable bribe, inspection or infraction.

My most treasured items while traveling through Mexico and Central America are copies of used Playboys. I don't read them; I use them as bartering chips. Well, okay, I might take a quick look at an article during times of boredom. "El señor policia, no tango mucho dinero por la propina pero tengo Playboys para usted." You should see their eyes light-up and the smiles that protrude from their machismo faces. Don't take any of last year's issues; I have already passed all of them out.

Mexican Auto Insurance

There's no if, and, or buts—purchase Mexican auto insurance! Most US insurance policies are not valid in Mexico. You can buy insurance near the border, or from AAA, it's not too expensive. The insurance is sold by the day and therefore you must estimate your entry and exit dates for Mexico. You may want to buy a couple of additional days of insurance for complications or unforeseen travel delays. If you have an accident in Mexico without insurance you could quite possibly land in jail until the matter is sorted out. The laws are different in Mexico and as a foreigner you must comply with these laws. At the very least, consider it insurance to keep out of jail.

Costa Rican Auto Insurance

Costa Rica is the only other country in which you are required to purchase auto insurance. The procedure is simple and straightforward. When you enter the country you must purchase insurance for at least one month. The price is of 1/2007 is $7-$20 per day. There is no need to make arrangement before the trip, the insurance is sold in the customs building at the border.

Auto Insurance In Guatemala, Nicaragua and Honduras

You are not required to purchase auto insurance in these countries. It is possible to buy auto insurance in Honduras for one year, see the Honduras section for details. If you decide to venture into Belize as a side trip, auto insurance is required—it's available at the border.

The Whole Shebang

You can purchase a policy from Sanborns for all of Central America and Mexico in the U.S. Call Sanborns for an updated quote at Toll Free (800) 222-0158

Gasoline

Always use high grade gasoline, regular leaded is second-rate and will clog your gas filter. Unleaded gasoline is available in Mexico, Guatemala, El Salvador, Honduras, Costa Rica, Belize and Nicaragua. You can expect to pay about the same per gallon as in the US (perhaps a bit cheaper) for Magna Sin, which is unleaded gasoline. In all other cases you always want to use Super or Extra.

In order to use leaded gasoline you'll need a funnel to put the gasoline in your unleaded restricted gas tank. If you are driving an older vehicle it is possible to remove the restricting piece at the opening of the gas tank. If you should find yourself with a tiny hole after removing the problem piece, put a screw, washer and nut tightly into the hole in order to close the opening. In most vehicles you can then put leaded gasoline in your vehicle without adjustment. Albeit when you put leaded gasoline into your vehicle you will burn out your catalytic converter. Normally auto service is not required, however, Mexican border mechanics are experts at hollowing out or removing the converter if needed—this is illegal in the US.

Finding petrol for your vehicle during late evening hours is not a problem. Most gas stations are open all night along the coastal route and your only logistical problem is finding your way in the dark, though it is possible. In some areas along the mountain passes, Michoacán and Puerto Vallarta especially, the fog can be dense. If this is the case, locate a large truck and follow it. The yellow and orange running lights on the truck will act as a guide through the fog. Please proceed with caution when driving in these extremely dangerous conditions.

Latin American Driving Habits

Mexican and Central American drivers make driving in the cities a bit frustrating for visitors from above the border. Obedience to basic traffic laws seems to depend upon if a policeman is watching or not. For example, if you stop for a red light the impatient driver behind you may honk his horn and inch his vehicle uncomfortably close to your rear bumper, he may even tap it. All the same, if you drive through the light and receive an infraction Señor Impatient is not going to pay the fine for you. Additionally, the lines that indicate traffic paths are quite frequently ignored— therefore drive defensively.

Signals

Turn signals take on a different meaning in Mexico. Often a left turn signal on the vehicle in front of you is a sign letting you know it is safe to pass. Flashing headlights while passing lets oncoming cars know what you are doing. Additionally, when cars traveling the opposite direction flash their headlights as they pass you it is a warning that the police or military are up ahead. This procedure is especially common in Costa Rica where the police are famous for their radar traps.

Daytime Driving

The unwritten law of driving in Central America and Mexico is don't drive at night. Most of the problems that travelers encounter take place on dark desolate evenings. As a general rule, get up early in the morning and drive until dusk. Although, it is very easy to drive into the night when a more preferential town is only one or two hours further. It is likely that you will break the night driving rule in order to find a good place to stay. There have been groups of people that have driven to Honduras in five days from California, they take turns driving and go continuously. For those adventurers that dare to be different, you could theoretically drive from the US-Mexican border to Costa Rica in seven days, (coffee aficionados).

Nighttime Driving

Challenging road conditions worsen at night; occasionally drivers do not use head-lights claiming that it is saving them gasoline. Additionally, animals and potholes in the roadway make driving even more dangerous at night. When driving at night, decrease your speed and use high-beam lights, respectful of other drivers—please! In many instances you will notice that nighttime drivers use their high-beams upon approaching your vehicle. Many times after you signal them to switch to a lower beam they don't because the high-beams are the only functional lights on their vehicles. When this happens focus your eyes on the white lines at the side of the road until they have passed. Also be aware that there is no highway lighting, thus when you add all the nighttime variables together -animals, potholes, high-beams, torrential downpours, the occasional bandit or military blitz—well, your odds are better at the roulette table in Las Vegas.

Finding petrol for your vehicle during late evening hours is not a problem. Most gas stations are open all night along the coastal route and your only logistical prob-lem is finding your way in the dark, though it is possible. In some areas along the mountain passes, Michoacán and Puerto Vallarta especially, the fog can be dense. If this is the case, locate a large truck and follow it. The yellow and orange running lights on the truck will act as a guide through the fog. Please proceed with caution when driving in these extremely dangerous conditions.

Animals On The Road

While driving you will encounter various types of animals: cows, sheep, horses, bulls, chickens, crows, vultures, pigeons, lizards, iguanas, snakes, rats, possums, deer, mules, oxen, coyotes, shrews, alligators, dogs, cats, and elephants. Well, maybe no elephants. I managed to avoid a collision with all of the aforementioned except a pigeon that I demolished in Mexico.

At first you will stop or come to a slow crawl when encountering animals on the road. Usually animals in the road will not move or cross your path as you drive by. Most of the animals are busily grazing by the side of the road and could care less about your presence. Therefore a slight variation in your path and a touch of the brakes will suffice. Do not stop for every animal that is on the road! If you do this you will never get to your final destination because animals are in the road con-stantly. More importantly, if you stop, the Latin American bus driver that is behind you will run you and the animal off the road without thinking twice. Of course, there are some instances when you will have to actually stop—use common sense, intelligence and caution—but don't be stupid.

Animals are your main concern when driving at night. Please note that some people in Latin America do not use their lights at night, thus never assume that a car is not rounding an invisible bend because there are no visible lights. Animals, on the other hand, never have precautionary lights, thus, you will never see them until they are directly in front of you. For your information, if you hit an animal of good size (cow, bull, horse, etc.) it is synonymous with colliding head-on with another vehicle. Be careful when driving at night!

Bugs

The biggest threat to your comfort on the trip into the heartland of Latin America is bugs. Yes, bugs! Spiders, mosquitoes and other various insects that crawl, fly, jump and BITE! In Mexico I fought a gallant battle with two small creatures. The following is my recount of a night that I battled the bugs:

After twelve hours of driving between Puerto Vallarta and Xtapa, I checked into a small clean quiet hotel one block from the ocean. I wanted to sleep, sleep, and sleep. After an hour I woke-up and my wrist was the size of a softball. Some creature—a spider that I happily disposed of later—bite me and created an intense immune reaction in my arm. After several minutes of contemplation, wondering whether the poison in the spider's venom would leave me to die in a hotel room thousands of miles away from my home, I decided that when it's time it's time, so I downed my last cerveza and fell back to sleep. To my disarray I awoke two hours later with what felt like multiple gunshot wounds on my back and arms. Mosquito! I did the usual window, screen and open crevice check before I accepted the room. I think mosquitoes can fly through walls. I was determined to find him. I tore my sheets off the bed, I pulled the bed from the wall, I searched every inch of the 12' X 12' room for my nocturnal intruder. During the search I managed to locate the spider that injected his love potion into me earlier in the evening. No red hourglass, great, that meant I wasn't going to die. I couldn't find my friend the mosquito, but I had to ensure that no future bites would take place. I took the portable high-powered fan in my room and strategically placed it as close to my bed as possible, and then I turned it on super turbo level 4. My intention was to create a wind tunnel that would deter any future landings by Señor Mosquito. Either the wind tunnel worked or the semi-poisonous venom from the spider availed me seven majestic hours of uninterrupted sleep. The lesson of this story is to never assume that the room will remain mosquitoeless (sic), therefore use coils or repellent before sleeping.

Toll Roads

You can expect to pay high toll charges as there are miles of new pay (cuota) highways in Mexico that have been privately built, though most Mexicans cannot afford the toll roads and they are eerily vacant. Generally there is a non-toll (libre) road going in the same direction for those that want to save money. The libre roads are often two lanes highways—one lane for each direction—that are crowded with commercial trucks and full of pot holes. Just the same, the fee roads will essentially take you to the same destination.

Speed Bumps Galore

You won't travel very far into Mexico before encountering speed bumps. They are called topes or bustos and they are located at the entrances and exits of small towns. Some are concrete blocks, others are iron bullets in a row and still others are a stretch of rises in the road called vibradores which give the car and everything in it a shiver and shake message. Topes extended high on the roadway may present problems for low riding cars. A loose tailpipe is especially susceptible to the speed bump phenomenon, thus a quick check and tightening before your trip may prevent problems. If not, you may spend a lot of time reattaching you tailpipe with chicken wire and sandwich twists. Check the fittings around the tailpipe before you depart as a precautionary measure, playing pick-up-the-tailpipe every one hundred miles along your journey is not an enjoyable game.

Auto Accidents

If you have an accident, stay calm, record all of the information that you can and wait for the local police. Get the other driver's license number and address. Do all the things you would expect to do in a similar situation in the US. In most cases it is the law and the custom to wait until the police arrive, even if no one is hurt. Do not move your vehicle after an accident, even if you are blocking a major highway. If you are driving a rental vehicle notify your rental agency immediately, let them take care of everything. You do have a responsibility to protect their vehicle until a representative shows up. Do not abandon it, even if it is incapable of being driven.

Should the vehicle be yours or loaned to you by a friend, then it is your responsibility to settle the situation. If the accident is your fault you must make payment right then and there (rarely do local drivers have insurance). If the accident is the other persons fault, you need to come to an agreement as to the amount of damage and collect from the other person—this is easier said than done.

If your vehicle is foreign registered and you have it in Latin America on a temporary permit, and the vehicle is permanently disabled, then you have a definite procedure to follow. In order to legally leave the country you must deposit the disabled vehicle with the proper authorities at the Aduana. You will be given documentation at the Aduana which will permit you to leave the country.

Carrying Merchandise Into Mexico

If you are carrying merchandise into Central America there are a number of additional concerns that require addressing, these are relatively new regulations and have been in effect for the last couple of years. There is a distinction between bringing personal possessions or gifts for friends and merchandise. Merchandise is listed as obvious items for resale. Even so, personal possessions may cause you problems if you have an overabundance of items.

If you are moving to Central America and you have decided that you want to take all the comforts of American life with you the border officials may consider the items merchandise. If you have merchandise it is necessary to enter Mexico at the border crossing just south of Brownsville, Texas. Here you are required to process Mexican paperwork, for a fee of $200—$300, and then you are permitted to travel on the Atlantic—Gulf of Mexico route, considered a gateway and intra-transit circuit. In most cases you have to transit with a caravan of trucks and commercial vehicles. If this is the case contact the Mexican Consulate for specific regulations and assistance. However, this whole procedure is complicated and bureaucratic, try to avoid it if you can because it's a real headache.

Gifts shouldn't cause you problems—all the same, if you add the custom officials and the military to Santa's List you can expect an easier passage.

What can I take into Mexico?

When crossing into Mexico, if you have no merchandise to declare, you must go through the Stop and Go light check point. A green light means proceed ahead without inspection. A red light means stop for inspection.

When you travel to Mexico by airplane or by ship, you are allowed to import (duty free) a total of items worth up to $300 per person (including children). For example, a family of five members consisting of the parents and three minor children can import up to $1,500 worth of merchandise, duty free. However, if you are traveling by land, you are allowed only $50.00 worth of merchandise duty free.

When you bring items whose value exceeds the above mentioned limits, but not more than $1,000.00, you can pay the taxes yourself. If your merchandise is worth more than $1,000.00, you must use the services of a customs broker.

If you are a resident in Mexico you are allowed to bring in free of duty the following items for your personal use: One camera or video camera if it can be carried by the passenger; up to 12 rolls of new film, video cassettes, or photographic materials; one article of sports equipment or a used set of equipment that can be hand carried; books and magazines; 20 packages of cigarettes or 50 cigars or 250 grains of tobacco; 3 liters of wine, beer or liquor (adults only); medicines for personal use or with a Doctor's prescription, if it is a controlled substance; and the suitcases to carry baggage.

If you are a resident of a foreign country (USA, Canada, or other), in addition to the above you are allowed to take a set of binoculars, a photographic camera, a television, a radio or radio-cassette, tape or disc player, up to 20 recording tapes or discs, a typewriter, a portable computer, a musical instrument that can be hand carried, a camping tent and camping equipment," a set of fishing equipment, a pair of skis, 5 used toys for minors, two tennis rackets, a motor less boat less than 5 1/2 meters long or surfboard with or without a sail.

If you are inspected and are discovered with items of greater value than is permitted and you have not paid duty on them, you risk having to pay a high fine (of up to four times the value of each item). If weapons or ammunition are found, the penalty could include imprisonment.

Products To Take into Mexico w/o Authorization:

.dehydrated or canned foods

.roasted coffee (packaged),

.fresh or dry meats (beef, sheep or goat from US or Canada) candy (not lactic)

.bamboo (dry)

.dried spices

.dry herbal medicines

.dry or preserved insects canned jellies or fruit preserves nuts

.straw articles or artisans dried fish

.cheese (processed in US or Canada) canned or processed sauces

.soups without meat canned or processed vegetables

.dogs or cats (with health certificate)

Leaving Your Car In Latin America

The following are the procedures for leaving your car in Honduras. The procedures are similar for leaving your car in Guatemala and Nicaragua. See the Costa Rican section for regulations on leaving your car in Costa Rica. Mexico has completely different regulations; remember, they have a bond on your vehicle until you return and therefore leaving your car in the country could be costly. The regulations are similar in each country with slight variations. In all cases you will be required to contact the Aduana and file the appropriate papers and pay the customary fees, officially. Theoretically, if you dump your car somewhere in the country and hop on a plane the authorities are not going to send agents to your home in the US. Notwithstanding, if you ever want to return to the country you may have problems.

Honduras, Specific Regulations: Suppose you drove a car to Honduras and then wanted to sell it or just leave it in Honduras and return by air. You will need to settle with the Aduana in order to be permitted to leave Honduras. This may be satisfied in several ways: payment of the import tax (by you or a purchaser), depositing the vehicle with the Aduana and receiving a receipt in which you may claim the vehicle (or what's left of it) at a later date, or ask the Aduana to extend permission to have the vehicle in Honduras for an additional 30 to 60 days during which a third party is expected to pay the tax or deposit the vehicle with the Aduana.

What do you mean I can't leave the country? When you entered Honduras with a vehicle, permission for the vehicle to enter was stamped in your passport. You must satisfy this permission requirement by driving the vehicle out of Honduras, paying of the import taxes, getting a third party extension, or depositing the vehicle with the Aduana. You have a 50% chance of being caught at the airport and not being permitted to leave.

Money Issues

How much money do you need for your trip into the depths of Central America? There is no one answer to this question. Be that as it may, travelers can expect to travel for far less than in North America or Europe. Everyone has a different level of comfort and you can expect to find accommodations for the total gamut. An average daily expense between $50.00 and $75.00 is a good target. You should first calculate the cost of gasoline for the entire trip and then prepare a daily expense budget for accommodations, food and miscellaneous fees, such as, entrance to national parks or museums. Border entries and exits should also be calculated. Some are more expensive than others, however, you can expect to pay around $100.00 for each country when all is said and done, including auto insurance where applicable.

Cash, traveler's checks, foreign currency, credit card—which should you take? Take them all! Cash is king, and US dollars are welcome everywhere. In fact, you must have greenbacks to enter Nicaragua. Take small bills and keep several one-dollar bills handy for the occasional propina contribution. Traveler's checks are bulky, inconvenient and not always excepted. However, if you get robbed you can get your money back if you properly recorded the serial numbers of the checks. Keep the numbers separate from your money and give them to a trusted soul before you leave as a backup. As a rule you should carry the majority of your funds in traveler's checks. A credit card is invaluable for emergencies. Plastic is accepted at numerous locations: gas stations, restaurants, hotels, service stations and super markets.

If times really get tough, you can also receive cash advances at most banks, however the fees are astonishingly high. Banks in Costa Rica receive 15%-20% of the total sum as a service charge. No card, no money, no checks...no problem! Call mom and have her send money via Western Union for a $50.00- $75.00 fee depending on the amount. Check Western Union here www.westernunion.com.

Buying a Car in Canada (For Non-American)

a) It is easier to buy a car in Canada than the US because of the ease of Insurance as a foreigner there. So if you want to drive Mexico or Central America, we recommend buying a car in Canada, adding an extra week driving down from Vancouver, for example, will make your life so much easier as you can just buy a car, get it insured as a foreigner in Canada---insurance is valid in the US---and drive on down to Mexico or Central America. We looked into rules to buy and get registration for United States bought car as a foreigner and decided we'd rather spend the months it would take do travelling.

b) If you enter by car into Mexico as a foreigner from the United States you need to go into the 'something to declare zone' to hand back your green United States visa card or else you will sail right through on green not knowing where to hand in the damn thing. (p.s personal experience means I now know you can hand this in at the foot crossing to a US official there but that means park in Tijuana and brave thousands of foot passengers in front of you to do so).

c) Make sure you learn to say "I am 'German/Polish/English etc..." in spanish. It is a faster ticket through any military checkpoint / awkward situation. You are not from the US---that is a bonus here---use it. Sorry for the US folk reading it, it's true. Hey you got the cool land, let us keep our benefits.

Gulf Route - An Alternative

Brownsville & Valle Hermosa, The Border

The roads on the gulf route are not nearly as bad as they used to be. The scenery is varied and beautiful. Depending on what time you cross the border into Mexico through Brownsville, you may choose to either stay in Valle Hermosa (Beautiful Valley) or continue on toward Tampico. Should you choose to drive all the way through to Tampico, I would suggest that you cross the border very early as this is a long journey. To make things comfortable, I would suggest you cross and get through the border town area as quickly as possible heading to Valle Hermosa. Please keep in mind that this border area is by far the "roughest" area that you will experience. You will definitely feel like you have entered into a third world counry here and you will want to keep your windows and doors locked if possible. There are many hotels in Valle Hermosa ranging in price. The one that I have stayed at there is safe, has secure parking, a café, and is only 17 dollars per night. It is a bit old and ran down, as are most of the hotels that you will find on your way south unless you are a high budget traveler. You are likely to be stopped at least 3 times after Valle Hermosa by either the military or the Federalis.

Brownsville to Tampico

The drive on into Tampico is rather desolate offering beautiful vistas. Please be advised that as of this writing, I would suggest that you not stop or pull over for any car behind you unless you have the experience and know how to identify that the vehicle asking you to pull over is definitely a government vehicle. There are some vehicles, that have been made to look "government". Be sure, be safe. Again, this is a desolate area. Keep your gas tank relatively full. I never allow the tank to drop below 1/4.

Tampico to Veracruz

From Tampico the next stop is Veracruz. Again, get an early start as this is a bit of a haul as well. If you start early both from Valle Hermosa and from Tampico, you will have a few hours of daylight left in Veracruz and in Tampico to enjoy the beautiful beaches and weather. From Veracruz, yet another early start. From there you will drive away from the coast headed Southwest toward Tierra Blanca. However, quite a ways before you get there, you will turn back southeast toward Cosamaloapan, then Acayucan. Pay attention to the beautiful cultural change that you begin to see through here. This is the change between native Mexican inhabitant culture and the Mexican culture that we American's are most familiar with. The area is definitely more agricultural, but I always find the people to be warm, friendly, and cooperative.

Acayucan-Arriago-Guatemala Border

I am not sure that this isn't my favorite area of Mexico. Spending the night in Acayucan, you can then make for Matias Romero and then east to Arriaga. Plan on a night in Arriaga. A few words about this town: this little farm town might possibly be the purest flash back to the 1950's in the United States that I have ever seen. There is no alcohol sold in the town after 7PM---so bring your own.

The town has a permanent carnival set up in it's center with little rides and booths. Children run the streets freely and safely at 10PM. The people are over anxious to lend you a hand in any endeavor you wish and it truly brings to mind how life should be. Again, the hotels are low priced and the food I definitely above average. If you happen to buy a hot dog from the hot dog vendor near the center of town, don't plan on eating it without making a mess. By the time he is done loading it up, it won't even come close to fitting in your mouth, all for about a dollar. From Arriaga, making it to the Guatemalan is a short skip and a hop and it is here that you rejoin the great original route offered by Gringo Travel Guide Pacific Route.

Mexico City in Mercedes

I made my trip no problem to Costa Rica a few weeks ago, I drove a 1983 Mercedes Benz Turbo Diesel. No mechanical problems what soever. It also helps I checked everything before the trip. Mexico was a beautiful country until we reached Mexico City to see the Pyramids. We got stopped 3 times be police and had to bribe about $200-300 dollars each time because they said foreign plated cars are not allowed in the State Of Mexico M-Sat 5am-11:pm or with plates ending with 0 or 00. I called 911 and eventually spoke to police officer that said it was true, but the fine was only about 1500 pesos—but the car would have to be towed until the fine is paid.

Entering Mexico City by vehicle takes some big cajones and lots of patience. I would recommend driving to Guadalajara and then take a bus or flight to DF, hang out for as long as you want, go back to Guadalajara grab your car and continue on your journey—this is a nice alternative and let's you visit DF in a relaxed manner.

Travel With Your Dog or Animal

If you take your dog through Mexico, no problem except some hotels don't like dogs. Crossing into Guatamala with a dog, no problem if you have a current health certificate. Crossing into Honduras, Grande problema if you don't have a VET waiting at the border! I had to make an appointment with the vet a week later and drive 10 hours round trip to pay him$ 60.00 for nothing but a stamp on a piece of paper. I think I could have dragged in a stuffed animal and he wouldn't have cared. Arrange to have a VET waiting for you at the border to get your dog into Guatemala.

Chapter
TWO
Mexico

I stopped in Mexico City on this trip and spend some time
in the city. This photo was taken in the zocalo, a must
place to see and hang out while in DF.

"Before God we are all equally wise - and equally foolish."
- Albert Einstein

Mexico is a vast and diverse country with hundreds of miles of beautiful beaches, high mountains, small pueblos, and huge cities. In fact, Mexico City is the largest city in the world. Moreover, the best thing in Mexico is not a place, it is the marvelous culture. Mexico is an extremely large country and you could easily spend months just traveling through the different regions. Don't expect the countries below Mexico to be more of the same, because they are not. Each country is distinctively different with its own culture and traditions. Enjoy the differences and respect each country for what it is, a unique expression of humanity.

Take some time and talk with the people, you will enjoy what they have to say. This book will take you down the entire Pacific Coast of Mexico and then through the mountains of Chiapas. The drive that is outlined in this guide offers detailed information on: Guaymas, Mazatlan, Puerto Vallarta, Ixtapa-Zihuatanejo, Acapulco, Puerto Escondido, Puerto Angel, Tuxtla Gutierrez and San Cristobal de Las Casas. You will see so many fantastically exquisite places in one trip that you will wonder why you hadn't taken this trip earlier.

These are the documents that you need to enter Mexico by car:

1. A tourist card.
2. A passport.
3. A temporary vehicle importation permit.
4. A temporary vehicle importation permit sticker.
5. Mexican auto insurance.

Border Locations, US—Mexico

There are several border entry sites between Mexico and the United States. If you are coming from anywhere in the west, southwest or northwest, the best entry location is Nogales, Arizona. You may also enter at Tijuana or Mexicali. Once in Baja you have two choices: (1) Travel Mex. 2 southeast to Santa Ana and pick-up Mex. 15 for the trip down the Pacific Coast; or (2) travel the 1,610k down the length of Baja California and then take a ferry to mainland Mexico at Santa Rosalia, La Paz, or Los Cabos.

Immigration & Customs

United States and Canadian citizens need only a Mexican Tourist Card for entry into the country. The paperwork for the Mexican Tourist Card is processed in the immigration office at the customs checkpoint. You must provide the immigration-customs officer with a proof-of-citizenship document. This is either a valid passport or a certified birth certificate (photocopies are not accepted unless certified by the proper issuing authority).

Mexican Tourist Cards are issued from 90 to 180 days. You need to present this to the customs officer in the customs building (oficina de aduana). The Mexican Tourists Cards are free, however I was told by the official in the immigration office that I must pay $6 for my Mexican Tourist Card.

Driving Through Cities

Most of the roads in Mexico go directly through cities and towns. Once you are in a city you must find your way through the city and on to your next destination. Find a large truck or bus that is transiting through the city and follow it. Trucks and buses move through the city and on to the highway using the most direct route. Thus providing a personal guide out of the city and on to the major highway.

Additionally, following large obstructing vehicles through the city provides cover for your gringo 'I am a target' .license plates and essentially the large trucks hide you from plain view. Obstructed, the city policeman, sipping his cold Corona, can not easily see your vehicle. By the time you pass his perch he rarely notices your smiling gringo face.

If you do get pulled over don't panic, remain cool and calm and get out some cash to expedite your continued journey—it doesn't take much, remember it's a negotiation so start very low.

Nogales, Arizona—Mexican Border

DRIVING TIME: 0 hours

KILOMETERS: 0

MILES: 0

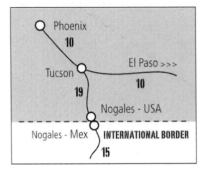

Initially you need to cross the border between the United States and Mexico. The officials at the border point will most likely look through your vehicle nonchalantly and then send you down the road to the main inspection area which is located outside of town.

The customs building is located about 24k past the main town on the outskirts of Nogales, drive directly out of town and follow the main road towards the city of Guaymas.

Learned Lessons

The regulation in which the officer claimed I had unlawfully broken was that I had in my possession more that two forms of recreational equipment. I was carrying my mountain bike, surfboard and a set of weights. The provision on the holy wall stated that travelers may only carry two forms of recreational equipment; thus, travelers that feel threatened by this provision are advised to contact the Mexican embassy before departing the US for further information.

Special Directions

Process your Mexican Tourist Card at the immigration office first and then proceed to the customs office—the two offices are located next to each other but the officials operate separately. The border checkpoint is not the place to process your documents, you must continue past the town of Nogales Once past the customs checkpoint. Follow the signs to Guaymas.

Don't forget your passport or your vehicle title, you won't be able to proceed on your journey without those two crucial documents.

Nogales, Mexican—Guaymas& San Carlos

DRIVING TIME: 6 hours

KILOMETERS: 421

MILES: 261

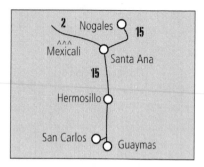

Guaymas is a good stopping point for the first night. There are camping facilities in San Carlos and plenty of hotels in Guaymas San Carlos is much smaller than Guaymas and more aesthetically appealing. It is located about 5k before Guaymas As you enter San Carlos there are several camp sites and trailer parks on both sides of the road with shower facilities and hookups for RV's. Don't forget your bug juice, the mosquitoes in San Carlos are the size of humming birds.

In the previous section daytime driving only is recommended. The following is a description of my nighttime escapade and I provide it as an example of why you should not drive at night:

Because of all the time that I had lost during the aduana fiasco in Nogales, I decided to make some time up and drive at night. Yes, I broke the first rule of driving in Mexico on the first night of my trip—perhaps I was fortunate to learn my lesson early. While driving through the coastal town of Guaymas, at approximately 3:00 am, I was pulled over by three policemen that suggested I had run a stop sign. I knew I was in trouble when I looked in my rear view mirror and saw a nice new Chevrolet pickup with police lights and three smiling faces.

If you have ever been pulled over by the police in Mexico you know that most police cars are several decades old and look as if the policemen push-start the vehicles to get to work in the morning. Albeit, when I saw this 1995 truck I figured that I would be the next contributor to that months truck payment. 'Infraction Senor, please show me your documents.' Though I objected and refuted the point that I had run the stop sign, I wasn't about to argue with three men with guns on an empty street at 3:00 am.

They were quite suggestive that since I had made an error that the Commander, driving of course, must be compensated for the infraction. The Natural Law Of Propina strikes for the third time in 12 hours. I went to my special reserves for this payment. See the section on Helpful Hints for details.

Learned Lessons

Don't forget to purchase bug repellent if you plan on camping anywhere along the coast. If you do drive through Guaymas at night look out for the Chevy police truck and expect a friendly visit with the local welcoming committee.

Special Directions

You may either stay in San Carlos or Guaymas San Carlos is located about 5k off the main highway before you reach Guaymas The road splits about 10k outside of Guaymas, it is well-marked with a large sign pointing the way to San Carlos.

Guaymas—Obregon

DRIVING TIME: 1.40 hours
KILOMETERS: 125
MILES: 78
HWY: 15

This stretch of highway extends into the mountains utilizing a road in good condition. The driving is straightforward without too much confusion. Once you leave Guaymas follow the signs for Obregon and Navojoa.

While I was driving along this section I was really tired and thus I pulled off to the side of the road, in the middle of a mud pit, for some shuteye. I slept for about three hours, after which I was awoken by the federal highway police. They said something indecipherable over the intercom and sounded their siren until I popped my head out of a window of my truck. I waived, smiled and said, "buenos dias." After several minutes of debate between the officers, they must have decided that it was too early to get dirty for some propina, they drove off, my luck was finally changing.

Learned Lessons

In retrospect, stopping in deserted areas is probably not too safe. Though in a long journey there are times when Mr. Sandman will not cooperate with the personal desire to continue driving. Therefore when you stop for a sojourner always stop at a gas station, restaurant or other luminous and populated location.

Special Directions

Going through Guaymas, turn right at the intersection before town and follow the signs to Obregon. If you miss the turn go directly through town and follow the coast through the port and industrial area. You will eventually encounter the road leading to Obregon. This is a bad road and goes through a nasty neighborhood and thus travel via the first road is recommended, although the second road is passable.

Obregon—Mazatlan

DRIVING TIME: 8 hours
KILOMETERS: 668
MILES: 415
HWY: 15

I had some bad vibes on this road. I stopped at what appeared to be a federal inspection station, (some of the upper states have inspection roadblocks when entering or leaving the state—however, I didn't run across any in the lower states after Puerto Vallarta), two men looking somewhat official came to my passenger-side door and opened it. After some introductions one of the two men opened the glove compartment and started rummaging around.

By this time I realized that this so-called official was not so official, thus I ended the conversation. However, this individual had already taken my flashlight and was thanking me for the regalo (present). I noticed that the other gentlemen standing around all had guns strapped to their sides, for this reason I gave the so-called present without objection.

As a side note, the toll road before Mazatlan is the best road of the entire trip and also the most expensive. Most tolls in Mexico cost between $2 and $4. However, this road cost $20. There is talk that this road is full of banditos because of the remoteness of the area. AAA has issued an advisory on this stretch of road and lists it as one of the most dangerous in Mexico. You have the option of a free road. Turn left before the toll road at Guamuchil, thus bypassing the toll road. This takes you through a much more populated area then the pay road, although it takes longer, it is considered safer.

Learned Lessons

Sometimes you can be overcautious. At no other time did anyone of official status approach my vehicle from the passenger side. Most, if not all, federal officers will have some kind of identification or a distinguishable uniform. Use caution and common sense and never pull over unless solicited by an official.

Special Directions

When you enter Mazatlan head toward the coast and you will find both camping and hotel facilities. Most hotels have guarded parking, notwithstanding, always take your valuables into your room with you. You might want to stay a day or two here, the beach is beautiful and the night life is especially good. Upon leaving follow the signs for Puerto Vallarta. You have a long day ahead so plan to rest well the night before your departure.

Mazatlan

Mazatlán is a Nahuatl word meaning "place of the deer." The city was founded in 1531. Mazatlán, with a population of 352,471 (city) and 403,888 (municipality) as of the 2005 census, is the second-largest city in the state (after Culiacán) and Mexico's largest commercial port. It is also a popular tourist destination, with its beaches lined with resort hotels. A car ferry plies its trade across the Gulf of California from Mazatlán to La Paz, Baja California Sur.

Mazatlan—Puerta Vallarta

DRIVING TIME: 8 hours

KILOMETERS: 462

MILES: 287

HWY: CA 15 & CA 200

Do not take the coastal road to Puerto Vallarta, it is the worst road of the entire trip. There is a fork in the road about half way between Mazatlan and Puerto Vallarta, stay on the road to Tepic and proceed to Puerto Vallarta via this route. I asked one of the highway police which was the shorter route at the fork in the road and the officer said that the coastal route was shorter. He failed to mention that there are about one hundred speed bumps and potholes.

The coastal route is about 100k shorter, however the roads are horrible and you pass through about 25 small towns. You are better off going to Tepic and than on to Puerto Vallarta. Note that just before Puerto Vallarta the time changes from Mountain Time to Central Time, add one hour.

Puerto Vallarta is a great town, you might want to take a short break here. Next to the restaurant La Pachanga is a guarded place for your vehicle and your belongings. You want to keep your eye out for places that offer board for vehicles as you enter these cities, in Mexico they are called pension para coche. Sometimes you can find a hotel that has gated storage or enclosures for your vehicle, but if you can't find a hotel there are usually gated lots that provide security for holding vehicles during the evening.

If you have a newer vehicle, or you are carrying a lot of nice things that you don't want to lose, always find a secure place for your car otherwise you may have nothing to return to in the morning.

* Pay the extra $3 or $4 for vehicle storage, it's worth it!

Learned Lessons

Don't take the coastal route to Puerto Vallarta. Follow the signs to Tepic and then proceed on to Puerto Vallarta. At Tepic the road splits from CA 15 to CA 200. From this point on you want to use CA 200 as a reference. Some travelers have reported that they follow the road to Tepic and then proceed on to Guadalajara. From Guadalajara they choose one of the several routes that empties on to the coast, CA 80, CA 110 or CA 37.

By the time you navigate your way through Guadalajara and drive back to the coast your driving time would be close to the same, besides, you don't want to miss Puerta Vallarta and the surrounding areas because they are undeniably magnificent.

Special Directions

When you first arrive in Puerto Vallarta you will encounter high rises, these are the major resorts. Don't panic! Follow the road straight to the central part of town and to the less expensive hotels. When leaving the city head south along the beach, next to the bus station turn right and follow the signs to Colima.

Puerta Vallarta—Ixtapa & Zihuatangjo

DRIVING TIME: 12 hours
KILOMETERS: 651
MILES: 405
HWY: CA 200

This potion of the trip is the most beautiful, the most dangerous, and entails the longest and most demanding driving. Dangerous because you are traveling through the mountains of Michoacan and the roads wind, twist and turn for the majority of the trip. You can expect your average speed to be between 40 and 50 miles per hour for the entire journey. Don't drive any faster! There are animals, potholes and speed bumps galore. Nevertheless, you will see some of the most awe inspiring coastline of the entire voyage, the beaches are radiant, powerful and peaceful and never seem to end.

This trip took me 12 hours with stops to use the bathroom and fill my gas tank only. I drove the last three hours of the trip in the dark. There are dangerous curves and extremely deep potholes that sneak up on you at night. If you have to drive at night, proceed with great caution.

Zihuatanejo is a relaxing coastal town with pleasant people, smiling faces and good food, is the fourth-largest city in the Mexican state of Guerrero. This town has been developed as a tourist attraction along with the modern tourist resort of Ixtapa, 5 km away. However, Zihuatanejo keeps its traditional town feel.[2] The town is located on a well-protected bay which is popular with private boat owners during the winter months.

Find a hotel with night security and good visibility. Enjoy the town and the beautiful bay, you deserve a break after the long drive from PV. Ixtapa is an expensive resort town located about 2k north of Zihuatanejo, its worth the hike or taxi ride to check out the beaches and night life.

About 1k outside of Ixtapa you will encounter a separation for Ixtapa and Zihuatanejo. If you are a high roller, take the road to the right into Ixtapa. Budget travelers should continue south along the main route another 5k into Zihuatanejo. At some point when you enter town you will need to exit the main throughway that runs through Zihuatanejo. Turn right and follow one of the several side roads down the hill which will take you to the beach.

If you encounter a small traffic circle veer right at the second exit and this takes you directly to the coast. There is an assortment of hotels situated near the ocean at economical prices.

Learned Lessons

This is an extremely long trip, but Zihuatenejo is an exquisitely beautiful town and it is a great place to hang for a few days. If you plan to make the long trip get an early start and fill your gas tank at every possible location. The city of Tecoman has several forks in the road, take the road to Playa Azul—not Pascuales. If you find yourself in Pascuales you have made a wrong turn in Tecoman, go back to Tecoman and find your way to Playa Azul.

Special Directions

The road is confusing after the first toll road. Stay on the road to Colima and exit the toll road at Tecoman. Always use the CA 200 sign as a reference and guide. Follow the cities and signs with the CA 200 reference and you won't get lost. In Tecoman take the road to Playa Azul, not Pascuales.

For Your Information & Enjoyment

The heart of Zihuatanejo is the waterfront walkway Paseo del Pescador (Fisherman's Path), also called the malecón. This tree-lined pedestrian walkway goes along the municipal beach between the archeological museum and the fishing pier. It is lined with restaurants offering seafood and many other dishes, as well as a variety of stores selling rugs, arts and crafts and souvenirs, and a small shell market. In the evening, this area fills with people socializing. Some of the best-known restaurants on this pathway are La Sirena Gorda Restaurant, Casa Elvira, which both specialize in Mexican and seafood dishes, the Mediterráneo Restaurant, which is noted for its pastas and fresh tuna, Daniel's Restaurant, which at times during the winter season features dinnertime music with happy hour all day long.

Ixtapa & Zihuatangjo—Acapulco

DRIVING TIME: 4 hours

KILOMETERS: 290

MILES: 180

HWY: CA 200

Leaving Zihuatanejo proceed up the hill out of town on to the main throughway. Follow the signs to Acapulco, you're still on CA 200. Going into Acapulco is a nightmare. The roads are horrible, the traffic is horrendous and there are literally thousands of people crammed into this coastal town. Nevertheless, there are many things to do and an endless amount of sun, fun and adventure.

Getting out of Acapulco is an art in itself. Pay close attention to these directions or you will get lost. Head south and up the hill, if you are near the beach you must drive up-up and away. Follow the signs for Mexico 95, this is the road to Mexico City and your passage to freedom. Once you work your way through the myriad of confusion you will come to an expressway that dissects the city. Get on the expressway and follow it south, follow any signs that display Mexico 95. Eventually you will see a sign for Pinotepa National, noted Pinotepa N. on the sign. Follow this road, this is the one you want for CA 200. Follow the signs to Pinotepa and then on to Puerto Escondido.

Learned Lessons

If you miss the original turn for Pinotepa National you can make a U-turn and backtrack to Pinotepa. The U-turn is about 2k past the original turn, there is a sign, so don't panic. Grab lunch somewhere in Acapulco and fill your gas tank, it's 8 more hours to Puerto Escondido.

Special Directions

Head south and up the hill, if you are near the beach you must drive up-up and away. Follow the signs for Mexico 95, this is the road to Mexico City and your passage to freedom. Once you work your way through the myriad of confusion you will come to an expressway that dissects the city. Get on the expressway and follow it south, follow any signs that display Mexico 95. Eventually you will see a sign for Pinotepa National, noted Pinotepa N. on the sign. Follow this road, this is the one you want for CA 200. Follow the signs to Pinotepa and then on to Puerto Escondido.

Acapulco-Pinotepa Nacional-Puerto Escondido

DRIVING TIME: 8 hours
KILOMETERS: 389
MILES: 242
HWY: CA 200

Okay, your on your way to Pinotepa National. When you first leave Acapulco the sensation is one of confusion as to whether your have chosen the correct road because there are no signs and you will pass through several small towns. Yet if you turned off the main highway and followed the Pinotepa N. sign you have nothing to fear except for the fact that the roads are wicked for several hours, after Pinotepa they improve greatly. This is a straightforward drive, about 8 hours with lots of potholes. Please be careful if you drive at night, read about my nocturnal adventure in the Learned Lessons section.

Hotel & Eats

In Pinotepa Nacional there is the Motel Carmona right at the entrance to the city. The place is always full and the big doors are shut tight until the morning. There is a cafeteria located at the motel. Time permitting, walk downtown and spend some time in the central part of the city, it is largely inhabited by indigenous Indians and it is a fantastic place to pass the time.

Puerto Escondido

PE is a great coastal town and those with some extra time might want to check out the gorgeous beach at Puerto Angel, about 45k south of Puerto Escondido. These are some of the most beautiful beaches in southern Mexico. If your not a strong swimmer you'll want to be extra cautious while swimming at Puerto Escondido. The surf is strong and the undercurrents are intensely powerful, it is know as the Mexican Pipeline. This is a popular surf location, I urge you to spend some time here whether you surf or not, it is a truly magical locale.

Hotel & Eats

Puerto Escondido has may nice hotels and restaurants, just look around and you won't go wrong. When you first enter town you will come across may roadside hotels. For the same price you can stay in a beach-front bungalow for $10—$15 US dollars per night.

Learned Lessons

Use extra precaution, you're now in the state of Oaxaca. Just outside of Pinotepa National I was followed for several miles, the car behind me shone an extremely bright spotlight at my vehicle as I left the town. Needless to say, I was concerned that I was in danger, it was 11:00 p.m. on a Friday night and I was in the heart of Oaxaca driving alone. My Toyota pickup reached elevated speeds and made perilous corners that I thought were only possible in a small sports car. Well, the Gods were good to me on this evening. The car following me had a stroke of bad luck after several miles and thankfully something rendered the car useless. In my rearview mirror I saw smoke spouting from the "bad guys" engine compartment. I can honestly report that I didn't travel at night for the remainder of the trip!

A Fork In The Road

At Puerto Escondido you may follow the coast to the Guatemalan border or you may enter from the mountains near San Cristobal de Las Casas. If you are not returning with your vehicle to North America you must travel to the border entry points at Talisman or Cd. Hidalgo in order to process your Mexican vehicle paperwork.

Special Directions

Fill your tanks in Acapulco, I almost ran out of gas before I made it to Pinotepa Nacional and I had an eighteen gallon tank. This particular area has almost no regular gasoline stations, be forewarned. For those that are desperate for gasoline, there are private enterprises along the route which will fill up a gasoline container at a cost 50% higher than normal or if you want to carry an extra 5 gallon tank with you this is where it would come in very handy. Make sure you place that container somewhere safe—you don't want it to become an explosive and the fumes can be super harmful too so only use a good container.

Puerto Escondido-San Cristobal de Las Casas

DRIVING TIME: 8 hours

KILOMETERS: 647

MILES: 402

HWY: CA 200 & CA 195

After leaving Puerto Escondido the roads are bad, in fact, from Puerto Escondido to San Cristobal de Las Casas they are extremely bad. This is a confusing drive so follow these directions and your maps carefully. You want to head for Salina Cruz and then for La Ventosa. At Salina Cruz the road changes to CA 185 for a short distance and then to CA 190, do not use CA 200 as a reference.

Most signs after Salina Cruz read both CA 185 and CA 190. The road forks at Tapanatepec, CA 190 leading to San Cristobal de Las Casas and CA 200 leading to the cities in the south: Tapachula, Ciudad Hidalgo and Talisman. For those traveling to San Critobal de Las Casas follow the signs to La Ventosa and then on to Tuxtla Guitierrez. After entering Tuxtla Gutierrez veer right and follow the signs to Chipa de Corzo and then to San Cristobal de Las Casas.

Learned Lessons

Be cautious driving through Chapias, you're in the heartland of people that have been struggling to preserve their identity for years. Before making the drive from Puerto Escondido pick up a newspaper or talk with a local Mexican to determine the present situation in the area. This region of Mexico is like no other, both politi-

cally and aesthetically. Pine trees, green forests and cool days permeate this stretch of Mexico. However, the greatest asset of this territory is the people. Chiapas is home to a large population of indigenous people. It's a wonderful place.

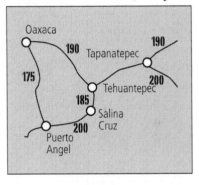

A Fork In The Road

At Puerto Escondido you may follow the coast to the Guatemalan border or you may enter from the mountains near San Cristobal de Las Casas. If you are not returning with your vehicle to North America you must travel to the border entry points at Talisman or CD Hidalgo in order to process your Mexican vehicle paperwork.

Special Directions

Don't forget that the road splits at Tapanatepec. If your heading towards the mountains your going the right way to San Cristobal de Las Casas. Those following the coastal route are urged to follow the signs to Tapacula. There have been some reports of banditos on this road so be careful and don't drive it at night.

* Quick Mexico Statistic: Population 109,955,400

Puerto Escondido-Tapachula-Talisman or CD Hidalgo

DRIVING TIME: 9 hours—2 hours from Tapachula to the border

Those individuals driving the coastal route should drive south from Puerto Escondido toward Tehuantepec on CA 200. You want to head for Salina Cruz and then for Juchitan and Arriaga. Stay on CA 200 and head for Tapachula and the border, see the map in next section. You can enter the border at Talisman or Cuidad Hidalgo. The drive along Highway 200 to Tapacula is picturesque. Beautiful scenic country, and an excellent road make this a pleasurable drive.

Learned Lessons

Sleep well the night before you cross the Guatemalan border, the officials have a reputation for complication, bureaucracy and indolence. If possible cross the border in the morning and allow yourself most of the day to deal with the crossing. Tapachula is the last city before you cross into Guatemala and you will find several excellent economical hotels.

If you arrive in Tapachula late in the afternoon stay the night in Tapachula. The reason is twofold. Primarily, you never know how long your border crossing will take and therefore you should avail yourself plenty of time. Secondly, if you are delayed at the border until dark you will have to travel deep into Guatemala before finding accommodations for the evening. Consequently, if you are forced to drive in the evening you may encounter the military or other undesirables while driving.

Guatemala is not Mexico and the two countries have nothing in common. There are far fewer tourists driving through Guatemala then Mexico and the possibility of encountering guerrillas is still probable—in this context the word guerrilla does not refer to the animal, it refers to the people with guns and lots of military-looking equipment.

A Fork In The Road

At Puerto Escondido you may follow the coast to the Guatemalan border and enter at Cuidad Hidalgo (the main crossing point on the international border with Guatemala) or you may enter from the mountains near San Cristobal de Las Casas.

If you are not returning with your vehicle to North America you must travel to the border entry points at Talisman or CD Hidalgo in order to process your Mexican vehicle paperwork, allow 2 hours, arrive early, not at lunch time, avoid weekends and public holidays.

Special Directions

Continue south out of Tapacula to either Talisman or Ciudad Hidalgo, both are entry points into Guatemala. Talisman is a smaller border crossing area with Ciudad Hidalgo being the major commercial entry point into Guatemala.

We recommend going to San Crsitobal, an amazing place and a wonderful escape from the heat along the coast. Additionally the crossing is much simpler and allows for a more relaxing crossing.

San Cristobal is located in the Highlands of Chiapas at an elevation of approximately 2100 m (6890 ft) above mean sea level. The city is named after Saint Christopher and Bartolomé de Las Casas, a Spanish priest who defended the rights of indigenous Americans and was the first bishop of Chiapas.

San Cristobal de Las Casas-Cuauhtemoc

DRIVING TIME: 2.5 hours
KILOMETERS: 170
MILES: 106
HWY: CA 190

Driving in San Cristobal de Las Casas is very agitating. There are several hotels on the out-skirts of town and everything is within walking distance of the center. A good place to sleep is The Maya. As you enter town, The Maya is located about two blocks past the Pemex station on the left. There are two big iron gates at the front, which are closed at night and avail excellent security for your vehicle.

Leaving San Cristobal de Las Casas, follow the signs for Comitan out of the city and on to Cuauhtemoc. Cuauhtemoc is located on the border of Mexico and Guatemala. Fill your tanks at any gas station you come across. When you see the iron gate across the road you are at the Mexican—Guatemalan border.

Hotel & Eats

The Maya costs 80 pesos, has hot showers and friendly service. There are plenty of great restaurants in San Cristobal de Las Casas. You are in for a gastronomic delight!

Learned Lessons

Those taking their vehicles out of Mexico and not returning to North America may not exit Mexico at Cuauhtemoc. You are required to process your vehicle paperwork at either CD Hidalgo or Talisman. However, those that are returning with their vehicles to North America can exit at Cuauhtemoc. Tell the border official that you will be returning to Mexico before your entry permit expires. Check your Mexican Entry Permit before leaving the country, most are valid for 6 months. A

Fork In The Road

At Puerto Escondido you may follow the coast to the Guatemalan border or you may enter from the mountains near San Cristobal de Las Casas. If you are not returning with your vehicle to North America you must travel to the border entry points at Talisman or CD Hidalgo in order to process your Mexican vehicle paperwork.

Special Directions

If you're at Cuauhtemoc and you need to process your vehicle paperwork, head back towards Comitan and catch CA 211, follow the signs to Huixtla. At Huixtla go south on CA 200 and cross the border at CD Hidalgo or Talisman.

Departing Mexico

KILOMETERS: 690—150k from Tapachula to the border
MILES: 428—106m from Tapachula to the border
HWY: CA 200—Guatemalan Border

Aduana

Checking out of Mexico is easy. Present your paperwork to the guard at the guard station immediately before the border. You won't miss the border, there is an iron gate blocking your entry into Guatemala. There are no signs, hence, just look for the gate.

This is a very informal border crossing compared to the others and is worth the extra couple of hours drive. When I arrived at the border I was the only car crossing, no lines and no hassles. The Mexican official will check your papers, ask you the usual questions, take a quick look through your possessions and then let you proceed.

Servico International de Fumigacion

Before leaving Mexico the fumigation police will spray your vehicle with a horrid smelling chemical. Of course there is a nominal service charge. You will need the fumigation certificate on the Guatemalan side of the border, don't throw it away. After fumigation, which takes about 5 minutes, you are permitted to enter Guatemala.

Currency Exchange at Border

There are always several black market currency exchangers located at the borders. You can't miss them because they are the only people holding large amounts of cash in plain view in Central America. You may exchange only enough to get you through the border and on to the next town or you can exchange enough money for your whole trip. If your plan is to travel through Guatemala directly to Honduras or El Salvador, it is best to change a sufficient amount of money for the complete day. There is no need to spend time trying to find and exchange money just to save a few cents. The rates are usually lower at the border, but on the other hand it's hassle free exchange. Latin American banks complicate foreign money exchange and most take their time when exchanging gringo money. Even though black market exchangers are illegal, officials won't hassle you when you exchange money with the exchangers.

Returning To U.S.

When you return to the US—Mexico border, before you cross, go to the Mexican vehicle check point. The officials will direct you to a Banjercito (Mexican Army Bank) office. Turn in your Temporary Import Permit and Vehicle Return Promise Agreement as well as your Tourist Card (FMT). Your vehicle security deposit will be returned or your bond agreement, depending on which method you used to enter. Of course you can just drive across without the formalities, and it's the simplest thing to do. But remember they do hold a bond on your vehicle. To avoid problems, take care of this before leaving Mexico or it will come back and haunt you. If you sell your vehicle in Mexico or forget to clear your credit card security you will be charged the value of your vehicle. What's your credit card limit?

Special Directions

When you return to Mexico several of the forms you used to originally enter Mexico can be used for your return trip. For example, the Tourist Card (FMT) and your vehicle security deposit allow multiple entries. These documents can be used for your return trip without getting new ones. If there is any doubt, check with the Mexican Consulate. You may purchase Mexican insurance for the return trip in Tapachula, located near the border.

Top Five Google Search For 'Mexico'

http://mexico-travel.com/

http://travel.state.gov/travel/cis_pa_tw/cis/cis_970.html

http://en.wikipedia.org/wiki/Mexico

http://news.bbc.co.uk/2/hi/americas/country_profiles/1205074.stm

http://www.visitmexico.com/wb2/Visitmexico/Visi_Home

Top Three Google Search 'Drive To Mexico'

http://www.mexonline.com/drivemex.htm

http://www.wikihow.com/Drive-in-Mexico-Without-Getting-Into-Trouble

http://studenttravel.about.com/od/getontheroad/a/mexicodrive.htm

Chapter
three
Guatemala

I came across this landslide on the road, there was no other way around—I had to wait a week for it to be cleared. You can't be in a hurry in Latin America.

"If you cannot get rid of the family skeleton,
you may as well make it dance."
- George Bernard Shaw

Guatemala is a fascinating country. The highlands are gorgeous and the vistas are absolutely breathtaking! The people of Guatemala have endured years of internal struggle, but you would never realize it from the smiles on their faces as you drive through the miles of farmland. There is little evidence of First World influence in Guatemala and, perhaps, this is what makes it so appealing.

Unfortunately, there are thousands of poor children in Guatemala. Take something to give to them, anything. Buy a box of chocolates or take some used clothing. Pull over when you feel compelled and give these people one of your gifts. The smiles that you will create are worth more than most any material possession you will ever receive. Of course, you can't give every child a gift. For those that you can give something, you have made a world of difference in the life of a special human being.

Immigration

Immigration is your first stop, you need an entry stamp which costs a few US dollars. Most Central American border crossings are rather informal and trouble free for the normal traveler. The problems and difficulties arise when you must clear your personal vehicle for passage into each respective country. You can expect to see the majority of non-vehicle travelers whiz right by you while you're patiently processing your monotonous paperwork. Don't get discouraged, and remember to wave to these other travelers as they board the bus with the chickens and pigs.

Aduana

Many travelers have reported that entering Guatemala is a pain in the @#!. Fortunately, I had no problems entering Guatemala. The officials were actually very amiable and courteous. They spoke more English than their Mexican counterparts and they were more helpful. I may have happened to catch them on a good day. The boss was sipping the Guatemalan drink of choice at his early morning break, and it wasn't just coffee. The atmosphere in the office was pleasant and casual.

Most travelers have reported that this is one of the most difficult border cross-ings in Central America. Many have had to spend three hours or more just to get permission to enter Guatemala. Be patient, provide the information required, pay the fees and eventually passage will be granted.

The officials want to see you passport, car registration, car title, and drivers license. After looking over your papers and then looking through your car they will give you a green document called Certificado De Vehiculos Automotors For Carretera De Placa No Centroamericano. The cost of this document is $6-10 US. Of course, there is also a form for Servicios Extraordinarios. This document costs an addi-tional $6-10 US.

Agriculture

This is a quick 5 or 10 minute stop. Show your fumigation papers to the semiof-ficial in the shack next to the Aduana. I paid a $2 US processing fee; the fee most likely varies depending on the type of car you drive and whether the official is exceptionally hungry or thirsty. The official records the information in a ledger and you are free to go.

Guatemala Border Crossing

TO GUATEMALA CITY
DRIVING TIME: 5 hours
KILOMETERS: 266 km

There are three main border crossing into Guatemala: Cuauhtemoc, Talis-man, and Cuidad Hidalgo. All three lo-cations basically follow the same entry procedure. The following directions are specifically for Cuauhtemoc.

Migracion, Aduana and Agriculture are located in three separate building that are next to each other. For your next stop you need to drive about 5 minutes down the road. The fun is not over yet!

Military Checkpoint I

On your way out of town you will come across the military checkpoint, look for the green uniforms. There is no building, the guards have a table set up outside next to the road. Park your vehicle and take your papers and identification to the guard. He will review your documents, ask you several questions and then record the information. No charge, this one's a freebie.

Military Checkpoint II

About 50K from the border there is a second checkpoint. Show the guards your paperwork and a friendly smile. They will question you and then, hopefully, let you proceed without propina payment.

Military Checkpoints, In General

There are several additional military-police like checkpoints on the way to Antigua. I was never solicited to pull over and therefore I didn't. Sometimes I received a stare or an intense look of interest. I always looked straight ahead and proceeded slowly past their building. Surely if you voluntarily pull over the guards would gladly search your vehicle and therefore request a donation for their work. My recommendation is to proceed with intelligence, caution and common sense. If you are solicited to pull over—always comply. Remember, a radio is much quicker than a vehicle.

Road Conditions

The road conditions in Guatemala are very good, however, there are few signs or road markers. Look carefully for the signs that do exist—if you miss one you may get lost. Also note the following differences for navigational purposes: CA 1 is the Interamerican Highway; CA 2 is the Ruta Pacifica and travels along the southern portion of the country. Hwy 1 is a separate from CA 1 the Interamerican Highway.

Special Directions

The officials want to see you passport, car registration, car title, and drivers license. After looking over your papers and then looking through your car they will give you a green document called Certificado De Vehiculos Automotors For Carretera De Placa No Centroamericano. The cost of this document is $6 US. Of course, there is also a form for Servicios Extraordinarios. This document costs an additional $6 US.

Guatemala Border to Antigua

DRIVING TIME: 5 hours

KILOMETERS: 288

MILES: 179

HWY: CA 1

After surviving the monotonous entry procedures for Guatemala the drive through the beautiful mountains and lowlands are refreshing. Keep your eyes out for any signs, you want to follow the one or two signs that indicate Guatemala, this is for Guatemala City. After several hours of driving you will see a sign for Antigua, turn right here and prepare yourself for a horrible road. If you decide to skip Antigua, which would be a crime, you may continue straight along the same road toward Guatemala City which is about one hour further.

Antigua is exquisite. Similar to San Cristobal de Las Casas, this city is confusing when first entering by vehicle. As you enter the city you will come to a fork in the road two blocks past the Texaco station, veer left at the fork. Approximately 1 kilometer past the fork in the road is Casa de Santa Lucia, between 5 and 6 Calles Ponienta. Santa Lucia is on the right side of the street, the entrance is a large black wooden door. If you go past the bank you have gone too far. Santa Lucia is one block before the bank. The parking area is located in the rear, but you will need to knock and ask them to open the gates. This is a very secure place, you want to take extra precautions in Guatemala with you vehicle—they frequently disappear.

Hotel & Eats

Casa de Santa Lucia is a nice place. There is a garden lounge great for mingling with other travelers. Rooms are $30 US + $5 US for storage of your vehicle. The bank, one block away, is open until 10:00 p.m. and it is a convenient place to exchange your gringo dollars. Turn right at the corner where the bank is located and walk 3 blocks to the center of town. There are several restaurants that offer delicious food—enjoy and relax.

* Quick Guatemala Statistic: Population 13,002,206

Learned Lessons

Be patient at the border and allow 2 or 3 hours to complete the necessary paperwork. If you are coming from San Cristobal de Las Casas allocate about 8 to 10 hours for the entire day.

Road Conditions

The road conditions in Guatemala are very good, however, there are few signs or road markers. Look carefully for the signs that do exist—if you miss one you may get lost. Also note the following differences for navigational purposes

Special Directions

Give yourself enough time to make it to Antigua from the Mexico-Guatemalan border. Please don't drive at night! Violence is a way of life in Guatemala and there are very few towns between the border and Antigua. The countryside is sparsely populated and there are few foreigners driving through the country.

Antigua-Guatemala City

DRIVING TIME: 1 hour
KILOMETERS: 52
MILES: 33
HWY: CA 1

The drive from Antigua to Guatemala City is very easy, it's Guatemala City that will give you a headache. This is your true test of patience, the only thing that will get you through is diligence. Unless you have specific business in Guatemala City, drive directly through it. In actuality you will drive around, backward, circular and then through.

The drive takes about 1 hour and once in Antigua you will find many places to store your vehicle inexpensively.

Guatemala City is the junction point for several routes leading to El Salvador or Honduras. It is possible to completely avoid El Salvador or you can drive through

El Salvador and then through a small portion of Honduras. One thing to consider is that if you decide to bypass El Salvador you are eliminating one additional border crossing.

Within the confines of modern Guatemala City is the ancient Maya city of Kaminaljuyu. Kaminaljuyu was first occupied between 1200 and 1000 BC and the city continued to be inhabited for about 2000 years before it was abandoned in the Late Classic Period of Mesoamerican chronology (600–900 AD). It is one of America's most notable archaeological sites. The center of Kaminaljuyu was located a short distance from the oldest part of Guatemala City. However, in the late 20th century, the city grew around the ruins, and, in some cases, over some of the outlying ruins before they were protected.

Many of the several hundred temple mounds have been built over with freeways, shopping centers, commerce, luxury hotels and residential areas. The central ceremonial center of Kaminaljuyu was however protected by the Guatemalan government and is now a park within the city. There are also many ruins still in existence, protected by the government.

Guatemalans have a diversity of origins, with Spanish and Mestizo descent being the most common. Guatemala City also has a sizeable Indigenous population and minority groups such as Germans and other Europeans, Jewish, Asians primarily Chinese and Korean, and many groups of other Latin American origins such as Peruvian, and Colombian amongst others.

Guatemala City is subdivided into 22 zones designed by the urban engineering of Raúl Aguilar Batres, each one with its own streets and avenues, making it very easy to find addresses in the city. Zones are numbered 1-25 with Zones 20, 22 and 23 not yet existing.

Special Directions

My recommendation is to find a nice relaxing hotel in Antigua and spend some quality time in this fantastic city. and travel to Guatemala by bus to see this city and the surrounding areas.

* Quick Guatemala Statistic: Guatemala won its independence in 1821.

Guatemala Border Exit

Regardless of whether you travel through El Salvador or Honduras your first procedure is to exit Guatemala. Leaving the country is much easier than entering the country.

Immigration
Immigration will request to see your passport and any other necessary documents. After the officials review your materials they will give you the exit stamp for $2 US.

Aduana
Aduana wants your vehicle papers, the green documents. The inspector will check your identification and your signature. He will then give you a stamped paper authorizing your exit from the country—kind of like a get-out-of-jail free card in Monopoly.

You must show the stamped paper to the nice military man that is patiently waiting to inspect every inch of your vehicle, good luck. After you get the okay from the military, the money exchanger guy will open the gate to let you and your vehicle out of the country—which is his side job, exchanging money or opening the gate?

Learned Lessons
The military and the government inspectors seem to operate completely independent from each other. When things run smoothly with one agency, don't expect the other agency to follow suite.

Special Directions
The exit procedures are straightforward, though you may get an attitude from the military inspector. He gives the final okay on exiting the country, thus treat him with respect.

To & Through El Salvador
For travelers going on to El Salvador there are several entry points; Las Chinamas, La Hachadura, San Cristobal, or Anguiatu. Ruta Pacifica, CA 2, will take travelers to the southern most entry point at La Hachadura.

The Interamerican Hwy, CA 1, branches just past Cuilapa into CA 1 and CA 8. CA 8 leads to the border crossing at Las Chinamas and CA 1 takes travelers to San Cristobal. There is also an entry point in the north at Anguiatu near to the Honduran border. Once you enter El Salvador it's a straight drive on CA 1 to Honduras. You can easily drive through El Salvador in one day.

To Honduras

Those going on to Honduras have two options. You may cross the border at Agua Caliente or El Florido. Leaving Guatemala City locate CA 9. Upon entering Guatemala City turn right on Puente Periferico and continue to Avenida Marti. Once you exit the city head for Esquipulas. It is entirely possible to drive from the Guatemalan—Mexican border to the Honduran border at Esquipulas in one day. However you do need to get an early start and keep driving without delay.

Car & Visa

You get a 90 day visa for your car as long as you have the TITLE in your name. You can NOT extend it. You must leave the country with your car for at least 3 days after the 90 days and then you can re-enter for another 90 days. If you overstay the 90 days you will be fined U$180.00 and be expelled. Also, tourists get a 90 day visa that can only be extended for 30 days at a whack and it is a big hassle to do that. So, you must also leave the country for at least 3 days and then return. However, when you leave—you must go to a country outside of the CA-4 (Honduras, Guatemala, Salvador, Nicaragua) for that period of time.

Guatemala City-Honduras Border

ENTERING HONDURAS AT EL FLORIDO, TO COPAN RUINAS
DRIVING TIME: 5 hours
KILOMETERS: 265
MILES: 164
HWY: CA 9—CA 19—CA 18—CA 10—CA 11
BORDER OPEN 8 a.m.—6 p.m.

Upon leaving Guatemala City locate CA 9. It's unimaginably easy to get lost around Guatemala City. After entering Guatemala City turn right at Puente Periferico and continue to Avenida Marti. Once you exit the city head for Esquipulas. At Quezaltepeque you can head north to Chiquimula and on to to El Florido or Copan.

The turn-off for El Florida is approximately 2 kilometers before Chiquimula. This is a dirt road that takes about 2 hours. During the rainy season this road may be impassable. I drove it in the late afternoon during a torrential downpour and I barely made it through in four-wheel drive.

Once you get to the border you have another 20 minute drive to Copan. There are very few signs on this route, so when in doubt, pull over and seek assistance. Guatemalans are friendly and helpful people, don't be afraid to ask for directions—it will save you time and effort. See the following section, Entering Honduras, for entry requirements.

Entering Honduras at Aqua Caliente or Esquipulas

DRIVING TIME: 4 hours
KILOMETERS: 227
MILES: 141
HWY: CA 9—CA 19—CA 18
BORDER OPEN 8:00 a.m.—4:00 p.m.

Once on CA 9 head for Jalapa on CA 19. Then on to Esquipulas, CA 18. Don't rely on road signs or highway numbers. If you need to pull over and ask use the next large city as a reference. If you're too late for the border at Agua Caliente, Esquipulas is a nice place to rest for the night. Don't forget that border entries may take several hours, therefore it's best to start early in the morning.

Hotel & Eats

Hotel Cristo Negro, an excellent place to stay the night and a short distance from the Honduran border, is located just past Esquipulas. If you have some free time, check out the Cathedral and the surrounding area in Esquipulas. During the evening the gates are closed at the Hotel Cristo Negro, thus if you arrive late just bang on the gates and they will open them.

Learned Lessons

On my trip I missed the juncture for Esquipulas and therefore I had to drive to Zacapa and back down to Chiquimula for the turnoff leading to Copan. When you get lost or turned around you can usually find an alternate route not too far out of the way. Always keep your map within view and remember to check it frequently.

Special Directions

Follow the signs very closely and keep an eye peeled for the military. Always be polite, serious, and respectful to the police and military—you are a visitor in their country.

Enjoying Guatemala

Guatemala's many Mayan ruins and colonial buildings are its most impressive architectural attributes. One of the most intriguing cultural aspects is the infinite and exotic variety of the handmade, traditional clothing of Guatemala's Maya population. The design of the women's colorfully embroidered tunics, capes and skirts dates back to pre-colonial days. Certain details of garment and design identify the wearer's group and village, and can also have multiple religious or magical meanings. Music and traditional dance also feature in many Mayan religious festivals. Spanish is the most commonly spoken language in Guatemala, and Roman Catholicism is the principal religion. Evangelical and Pentecostal Christian denominations have gained wide followings, while the Maya have preserved aspects of their traditional religions, often blended with Catholicism.

Guatemalan cuisine can't compete with that of Mexico, although standard Mexican fare such as tortillas and tacos can be found. Mostly you'll encounter tough grilled or fried meat and more, yea, meat. Beans and rice are often the cheapest and best alternative, and the country has a surprising number of Chinese restaurants. Coffee is available everywhere—sometimes spectacularly good, but the best beans are typically exported. Beer is prevalent, in light and dark versions, and rum and

Quetzalteca are the nation's favored rocket fuels.

Guatemala City

Guatemala City is the largest urban agglomeration in Central America—it's far from a pretty site. It sprawls across a range of flattened, ravine-scored mountains, covering an entire mountain plain and tumbling into the surrounding valleys. With its rickety chicken buses and chaotic marketplaces, the city's Latin character is over the top to the point of cliché. Like all Guatemalan towns, a strict grid system has been imposed on the city's layout: avenidas run north-south; calles run east-west. The huge city has been divided into 15 zones, each with its own version of this grid system.

Few colonial buildings grace the city, and it is visited more for its role as the nation's administrative and transport hub than as a must-see tourist site. In Zona 1, Plaza Mayor is a classic example of the standard Spanish colonial town-planning scheme, and is the city's ceremonial center, with the retail district nearby. It's best visited on a Sunday, when it's thronged with thousands of locals who come to stroll, eat ice cream, smooch on a bench, listen to boom-box salsa music and ignore the hundreds of trinket vendors. The square is lined by the imposing Palacio Nacional, currently being restored to house a national history museum, and the twin-towered Catedral Metropolitana. An earthquake destroyed the original market building adjacent to the square in 1976, and today the hugely chaotic Mercado Central specializes in tourist-oriented crafts.

North of Zona 1 is the shady and restful Parque Minerva, featuring a quirky relief map of the country. Several important museums can be found in Zona 10, including the Museo Popol Vuh, which is a superb private collection of Mayan and Spanish colonial art, and the Museo Ixchel, which displays the rich traditional arts and costumes of Guatemala's highland towns. Zona 13 houses the Museo Nacional de Arqueología y Etnología, with its prized collection of Mayan artifacts, and the Museo Nacional de Arte Moderno, which has a superb collection of 20th-century Guatemalan art. Several km west of the center lie the extensive ruins of Kaminaljuyú, an important Late Pre-classic/Early Classic Maya site. Unfortunately, the ruins have been largely covered by urban expansion.

Most of the city's cheap and middle-range hotels are in Zona 1, while posh hotels are clustered in Zona 10. Zona Viva is the place to go to eat expensively and dance the night away.

Antigua Guatemala

Antigua was the nation's capital from 1543 until 1776 (following the devastating earthquake), when the capital was moved 45km (28mi) to the east to the present site of Guatemala City. Antigua is among the oldest and most beautiful cities in the Americas. Set amid three magnificent volcanoes—Agua, Fuego and Acatenango—its superb yet sturdy colonial buildings have weathered 16 earthquakes and numerous floods and fires. Antigua is especially beautiful during Semana Santa, when the streets are carpeted with elaborate decorations of colored sawdust and flower petals.

The city's churches have lost much of their Baroque splendor, the post-earthquake repair and restoration leaving them denuded of embellishment and elegance. However, many remain impressive, in particular La Merced, the Iglesia de San Francisco and the Las Capuchinas (now a museum). Casa K'ojom is a fascinating museum of Mayan music and ceremonies and related artifacts. On Sundays, visitors and locals alike gather to assess the goods for sale at the bustling market held in Parque Central.

Chichicastenango

At 2030m (6658ft), the magical and misty highlands town of Chichi is surrounded by valleys and overshadowed by looming mountains. Though isolated, it's always been an important market town. The Sunday market is the one to catch, as the cofradías (religious brotherhoods) often hold processions on that day. The locals have combined traditional Mayan religious rites with Catholicism; the best places to witness these old rites are around the church of Santo Tomás and the shrine of Pascual Abaj, which honors the Mayan earth god.

Incense, food and drink are offered to ancestors and to ensure the continued fertility of the earth. The town's Museo Regional contains ancient clay pots and figurines, flint and obsidian spearheads, maize grindstones and an impressive jade collection.

Quetzaltenango

The commercial center of southwestern Guatemala, Quetzaltenango, more commonly called Xela ('SHAY-lah'), is an excellent base for excursions to the many nearby villages, noted for their hot springs and handicrafts. The city prospered during the 19th century as a coffee-brokering and storage center until an earthquake and volcanic eruption ended the boom. In recent years, Xela has become well-known for its Spanish-language schools. The town's major sights are the central square and the buildings which surround it, a couple of basic though useful markets and the ubiquitous Parque Minerva—many such monuments were built during the presidency of Manuel Estrada Cabrera (1898-1920), to honor the classical goddess of education in the hope of inspiring Guatemalan youth to new heights of learning. The beautiful volcanic countryside surrounding Xela features natural steam baths at Los Vahos and Fuentes Georginas. Also in the vicinity is the picture-postcard village of Zunil, the garment district of Guatemala, San Francisco El Alto and the center for wooly woolens, the village of Momostenango.

Flores

The capital of the jungle-covered northeastern department of El Petén, Flores is built on an island on Lago de Petén Itzá, and is connected by a 500m (1640ft) cause way to the service town of Santa Elena on the lakeshore. Flores is a dignified capital, with its church and government building arranged around the main plaza, which crests the hill in the center of the island. The city was founded by the Itzáes, and at the time of conquest was perhaps the last still-functioning Mayan ceremonial center in the country. The pyramids, temples and idols were destroyed by the God-fearing Spanish soldiers, and the dispersal of the Mayan citizens into the jungle gave rise to the myth of a 'lost' Mayan city. Modern sights include boat rides stopping at various lagoon settlements and a visit to the limestone caves of Actun-Can.

Panajachel

Don't be deterred by this town's nickname of Gringotenango ('place of the foreigners'), nor by the town's lack of colonial architecture or colorful market. The attraction here is the absolutely gorgeous caldera lake (a water-filled collapsed volcanic cone). Since the hippie-dippie days of the 1960s, laid-back travelers have flocked here to swim in Lago de Atitlán and generally chill out. Volcanoes surround the lake, and the town is the starting point for excursions to the smaller, more traditional indigenous villages on the western and southern shores of the lake. The most popular day-trip destination is Santiago Atitlán, with its colorfully dressed locals and a unique, cigar-smoking resident deity called Maximón. The market town of Sololá has been attracting traders for centuries, and the town's main plaza continues to throb with activity on market days. Village life can be sampled at Santa Catarina Palopá, while lakeside San Pedro La Laguna is perhaps more attractive because it is less visited.

Tikal

The monumental Mayan ceremonial center at Tikal lies northwest of Flores in the department of El Petén. Its jungle location makes it a unique site. Towering pyramids rise above the jungle's green canopy, while down below howler monkeys swing nosily through the branches of ancient trees, colorful parrots squawk and dart, and tree -frogs fill in the auditory gaps. The steep-sided temples rise to heights of over 44m (144ft), and although the undergrowth around them has been cleared, the dense rain forest canopy is not far away, making passage within the enigmatic site an unforgettable experience. The many ruins include plazas, an acropolis, pyramids, temples and a museum.

Top Five Google Search For 'Guatemala'

> http://en.wikipedia.org/wiki/Guatemala
> http://www.state.gov/r/pa/ei/bgn/2045.htm
> http://news.bbc.co.uk/2/hi/americas/country_profiles/1215758.stm
> http://www.visitguatemala.com/web/index.php?lang=english
> http://www.lonelyplanet.com/guatemala

Top Three Google Search 'Drive To Guatemala'

> http://jalopnik.com
> http://www.travelblog.org
> http://www.lonelyplanet.com/thorntree/thread.jspa?threadID=1925476

Chapter four
Honduras

Things don't always go as planned, we sunk the vehicle to the frame and had to pay a local farmer $100 to pull it out with his tractor.

"Your friend is the man who knows all about you and still likes you."
- Elbert Hubbard

T he people of Honduras are extraordinary. You can always expect a smile and a friendly warm embrace wherever you go. Like most of the countries in this region the majority of the people are poor.

Honduras is a country stuck in time, not succumbing to the ideals and fast-paced occidental societal pressures that have taken other Central American countries by surprise. Take some time and mingle with the people, you will never forget their warm hearts and giving personalities.

Driving within Honduras is quite pleasant. The majority of the roads are very good, except for the road leading to and away from Copan. The police and the military do not bother you too much.

There are several police checkpoints and sometimes the police and the military run roadside blitzes. Always travel with your paperwork.

Mayan Ruins

While you are in Honduras take the time to enjoy this unique part of the world. However you choose to enter, plan a day at the Mayan ruins of Copán. If you entered at the Aqua Caliente border crossing continue on past Santa Rosa de Copán to La Entrada. Turn left at the La Entrada junction and continue toward Copán, the turn off is almost immediately after entering this city of La Entrada. From here it is about a two hour drive. The road is generally good and paved except for a very small section as you near the ruins.

In September 1996 a new spectacular museum opened on the grounds of the Copán's ruins. This museum is considered to be the foremost in Central America. The entry way is like a portal, something like you would see at Copán's Temple 22. Inside the museum are numerous serpent carvings, the Rosalila excavations and currently the Copán stela originals are being brought into the museum for preservation—don't miss this spectacular exhibition.

Entering Honduras

Driving within Honduras is quite pleasant. The majority of the roads are very good, except for the road leading to and away from Copan. The police and the military do not bother you too much. There are several police checkpoints and sometimes the police and the military run roadside blitzes. Always travel with your paperwork.

Immigration & Aduana

Same procedure, proceed to immigration and receive your entry visa and stamp, $2 US. Aduana will request the usual paperwork and identification: passport, car registration, car title, and driver's license. The officers will then type a Permiso De Entrada—Salida Temporal and Fuerzas Armadas De Honduras. These forms will allow you and your vehicle passage in Honduras for 30 days, cost is $30 US. There is another form that lists about 50 miscellaneous items the officers may fill-in for additional charges.

If you plan to stay in Honduras for longer than 30 days you must go to the Transit Police station and Migration office before the expiration date in order to secure an extension. This extension may be for up to six months.

Military

Next you must pass a military inspection, $2 US for the transit permit. Show the officer your documents and passport. He will check them along with your personal belongings and then let you proceed when he feels that all the regulations are fulfilled. Military inspections always seem to be the most tedious and difficult—have patience and don't forget to smile.

*Quick Honduras Statistic: Honduras became an independent nation in 1821. After two and a half decades of mostly military rule, a freely elected civilian government came to power in 1982.

Copan to San Pedro Sula

DRIVING TIME: 3 hours
KILOMETERS: 171
MILES: 106
HWY: CA 1

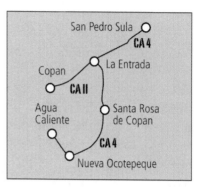

From Copan head towards La Entrada, about a one hour drive. At La Entrada you can travel on to San Pedro Sula or turn right towards Santa Rosa de Copan. Please note that Santa Rosa de Copan is different from Copan and the department (equivalent to a county or province) that you are in, which is called Copan. Therefore, when asking for directions be specific.

Copan to San Pedro Sula will take you approximately 3 hours. There are many places to stay in San Pedro Sula—make sure you park your car in a Parqueo for safety, car theft is notorious in San Pedro Sula. There are several parqueos next to Central Plaza and the Gran Hotel Sula—use them!

From Esquipulas to San Pedro Sula

DRIVING TIME: 4 hours
KILOMETERS: 235
MILES: 146
HWY: CA 1

From Esquipulas head for Santa Rosa de Copan. At Santa Rosa de Copan, you can go on to San Pedro Sula via La Entrada. The first few hours will take you through breathtaking mountains; after passing Santa Rosa de Copan follow the signs for La Entrada. An alternate route is to head toward La Esperanza and then on to Tegucigalpa, the capital of Honduras.

Learned Lessons

Don't drive these roads at night. There are many animals along the road and theft is common around La Entrada. Most of the roads are very good and you can expect to maintain a comfortable speed. Nevertheless, remember that you are sharing the roadway with children, livestock, carts and parked vehicles—take your time and enjoy the scenery.

Special Directions

The route via La Entrada and San Pedro Sula is visually stimulating and the roads are in great condition. If you want to visit the coast or the Bay Islands, this is the route to take.

Copan

While you are in Honduras take the time to enjoy this unique part of the world. However you choose to enter, plan a day at the Mayan ruins of Copán. If you entered at the Aqua Caliente border crossing continue on past Santa Rosa de Copán to La Entrada.

Turn left at the La Entrada junction and continue toward Copán, the turn off is almost immediately after entering this city of La Entrada. From here it is about a two hour drive. The road is generally good and paved except for a very small section as you near the ruins.

Copán is an archaeological site of the Maya civilization located in the Copán Department of western Honduras, not far from the border with Guatemala. It was the capital city of a major Classic period kingdom from the 5th to 9th centuries AD. Little is known of the rulers of Copán before the founding of a new dynasty with its origins at Tikal in the early 5th century AD, although the city's origins can be traced back to the Preclassic period. After this, Copán became one of the more powerful Maya city states and was a regional power in the southern Maya region, although it suffered a catastrophic defeat at the hands of its former vassal state Quirigua in 738, when the long-ruling king Uaxaclajuun Ub'aah K'awiil was captured and beheaded by Quirigua's ruler K'ak' Tiliw Chan Yopaat (Cauac Sky). Although this was a major setback, Copán's rulers began to build monumental structures again within a few decades.

This gorgeous village with cobbled streets passing among white adobe buildings with red-tiled roofs and small cafes is 1km from the famous Maya ruins. As you pass the ruins drive around the curve and into the heart of the town. The village has a lovely colonial church and a timeless pace, everything slows down in Copan.

The archaeological site at the ruins is open daily and includes the Stelae of the Great Plaza, portraying the rulers of Copán, dating from 613; the ball court and hieroglyphic stairway; and the Acropolis, which has superb carved relics of the 16 kings of Copán.

There are hot springs a one-hour drive from the village, and the nearby picturesque mountain village of Santa Rita de Copán has a beautiful plaza and a peaceful colonial church.

San Pedro Sula—Tegucigalpa—Choluteca

DRIVING TIME: 6 hours
KILOMETERS: 330
MILES: 204
HWY: CA 1

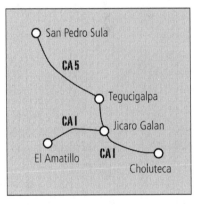

The splendid drive between San Pedro Sula to Tegucigalpa (or Tegus) takes about 4 hours. You will pass through miles of pineapple fields as you ascend into the mountains that surround this beautiful area.

Tegucigalpa, as a colonial city, has several barrios in the oldest districts of the city and Comayaguela, and colonias in the new ones. None of them have well-defined limits or even town-centers. There are some boulevards, none of which reach into downtown. Like in most Central American cities, there doesn't seem to be much rhyme or reason as to how streets are named, making orientation and driving rather difficult to first-time visitors to the city. Tegucigalpa was founded by Spanish settlers as Real Villa de San Miguel de Heredia de Tegucigalpa on September 29, 1578 on the site of an existing native settlement. Before and after independence, the city was a mining center for silver and gold. The capital of the independent Republic of Honduras switched back and forth between Tegucigalpa and Comayagua until it was permanently settled in Tegucigalpa in 1880, (see end of chapter for more info on Tegus).

Colonia Palmira, a wealthy neighborhood to the east of the city center on the Boulevard Morazan, hosts many of the foreign embassies as well as upscale restaurants. Lomas del Guijarro, Loma Linda and El Hatillo are upscale neighborhoods that house most of the apartment complexes in the city. The leading hotels of the city are found around these districts too. These include: Mariott Hotel, Clarion Hotel, Hotel El Centenario, Intercontinental, Honduras Maya, Plaza Del Libertador, Plaza San Martín, Hotel Alameda, Excelsior Hotel and Casino.

At Tegus head through town and follow the signs for Choluteca, CA 1. This is a 2 hour drive descending from the mountains.

As you drive this route there are a lot of things to see which may perk your interest. There are small shops situated along the road which offer fruits, candy and pottery particular to each distinctive region. The fruits are particularly delicious and shamefully inexpensive, pick some up for lunch.

If your stomach is rumbling, stop at one of the fifty or so restaurants located along Lago de Yojoa for a delicious and an economical fish meal. A few miles past the lake you can explore underground caverns at Las Cuevas de Taulabe.

About 20 miles before you reach Tegucigalpa there is a picnic area and zoo called Parque Aurora. This is a great place to stop and rest before entering Tegus.

Learned Lessons

Follow the highway through Tegus and head toward Choluteca. There are plenty of gas stations outside the city on the San Pedro Sula—Tegus route, thus don't worry about filling up in San Pedro Sula. However, fill up before you leave Tegucigalpa because there are few stations between Tegus and Choluteca.

If you need to exchange money before entering Nicaragua, do so in Tegucigalpa. Very few places in Nicaragua will exchange travelers cheques. Don't forget that you must have US DOLLARS for your entry into Nicaragua!

Special Directions

Follow the signs leading out of San Pedro Sula toward Tegus. You can expect thick fog in the upper mountain regions, thus watch your speed and take special precaution if you are driving at night.

Choluteca, Honduras—Nicaragua Border

DRIVING TIME: 1 hours
KILOMETERS: 58
MILES: 36
HWY: CA 1

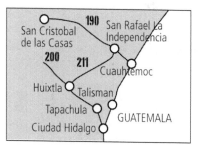

From Choluteca you may cross the border into Nicaragua via Guasaule or El Espino. If you want to visit the beaches in northern Nicaragua, head for the frontera at Guasaule.

For those traveling to Managua, Costa Rica, or the southern beaches, head for the frontera at El Espino. Further north their is also a border crossing at Los Manos.

Lessons Learned

You can expect a headache when entering Nicaragua. After leaving Tegu you will descend from the mountains into a hot, dry valley. There are several twists and turns in the road, thus after you leave Choluteca head for the appropriate border city (depending on your route in Nicaragua). Choluteca is the junction point for Guasaule or El Espino.

The main border crossing between Honduras and Nicaragua is at Los Manos. You may cross at any of the three sites depending on your travel destination in Nicaragua. Surfers will want to cross at El Espino and head for the beaches in the north. There are some great breaks near the city of Leon. The most popular break is at Poneloya.

Special Directions

If you find yourself at El Espino and you want to visit the northern beaches, head for Leon at San Isidro when you cross into Nicaragua.

Departing Honduras

Upon reaching the border you will be inundated by local people. Several are moneychangers and others are guides. Guides, I didn't want to take a trek through the jungle? The guides, which are non-official unemployed locals, will hold your hand and take you through the bureaucratic process at the border. I highly recommend hiring a guide, they are not expensive and their help is well-worth the money!

Find a guide that looks trustworthy, you can expect to pay between $10—$20 US. Offer half of whatever fee is requested. My guide requested $20 US for her services, we agreed on $10 US. The guide will take all of your documents to the Honduran border offices.

Eventually the guide will return with a Honduran official and he will ask the usual questions and take a look at your vehicle. The official will then give you the official OK to leave the country. Then the guide will take you into the Honduran Aduana building where you must pay an exit fee of $2 US. This procedure is somewhat confusing, but with the guide all will go well.

Lastly, hand your stamped papers to the gatekeeper and you're on your way to Nicaragua. Hopefully you have had a good nights rest because your head's going to spin; Nicaragua is a bureaucratic nightmare.

Learned Lessons

Bargain with the guides and always offer half the asking price for their services, or less if the fee seems exorbitantly high. Theoretically you don't need a guide, but they make the process much easier and hassle-free.

Special Directions

Double check your papers and passport for proper exit and entry stamps when the guide or official returns it to you.

Enjoying Honduras

Tegucigalpa

The capital of Honduras is a busy, noisy city nestled into a bowl-shaped valley nearly 1000m (3280ft) above sea level. It has a fresh and pleasant climate, and the surrounding ring of mountains is covered in pine trees. The name Tegucigalpa means 'silver hill' in the local dialect, and it was bestowed when the Spanish founded the city as a mining center in 1578.

Fortunately, the locals call the city Tegus for short, saving foreigners the embarrassment of mispronouncing the full name. Tegucigalpa became the capital in 1880 and, in 1938, the nearby settlement of Comayagüela was incorporated into the city.

The focus of the city is the domed 18th-century cathedral, which has a baroque interior full of fine art. Parque Central, in front of the cathedral, is the hub of the city. Interesting buildings include the old university, Antiguo Paraninfo Universitaria, now an art museum; the modern Palacio Legislativo, which is built on stilts; the Casa Presidencial; and the 16th-century Iglesia de San Francisco, the first church built in Tegucigalpa.

The city is divided by the Río Choluteca. On the east side is Tegucigalpa, with the city center and more affluent districts; across the river is Comayagüela, a poorer, dirtier market area with lots of long-distance bus stations and cheap hotels. It is cleaner, safer and more pleasant to stay in Tegucigalpa, although popular wisdom says it's cheaper in Comayagüela. If you do stay in Comayagüela, it's very dangerous to walk through the market area at night. The main area for budget accommodations in

Tegucigalpa is a few blocks east of the Parque Central; in Comayagüela, the best cheap hotels are around the El Rey and Aurora bus stations, between 8a and 9a Calles. Most of the good restaurants are on the Tegucigalpa side of the river, but Comayagüela has plenty of cheap Chinese restaurants. In Tegucigalpa, Boulevard Morazán and Avenida Juan Pablo II are the main nightlife areas.

Around Tegucigalpa

There are plenty of attractions around Tegucigalpa, including the huge Gothic Basílica de Suyapa, 7km (4mi) southeast of the city center. The Virgen de Suyapa, patron saint of Honduras, is believed to have performed hundreds of miracles. Santa Lucia, 13km (8mi) east of the city, is a charming old Spanish town with meandering lanes and a beautiful church. Valle de Angeles, 11km (7mi) past Santa Lucia, is an old Spanish mining town restored to its 16-century appearance. La Tigra National Park, northeast of the city, is one of the most beautiful places in Honduras. Located at an altitude of 2270m (7446ft), the pristine 7482-hectare (18,480-acre) park preserves a lush cloud forest that is home to ocelots, pumas, monkeys and quetzal.

Comayagua

Comayagua was the capital of Honduras from 1537 to 1880, and retains much evidence of its colonial importance. The cathedral in the center of the town is a gem. Built between 1685 and 1715, it contains much fine art and boasts one of the oldest clocks in the world. The clock was made over 800 years ago by the Moors for the palace of Alhambra in Seville, and was donated to the town by King Philip II of Spain. The first university in Central America was founded in Comayagua in 1632 in the Casa Cural, which now houses the Museo Colonial. The museum has religious art spanning four centuries of colonial rule. Comayagua's first church was La Merced, built between 1550 and 1558; other fine churches include San Francisco (1584) and La Caridad (1730).

Copán Ruinas

This beautiful village with cobbled streets passing among white adobe buildings with red-tiled roofs is 1km from the famous Maya ruins of the same name. The village has a lovely colonial church and an aura of timeless peace. The archaeological site at the ruins is open daily and includes the Stelae of the Great Plaza, portraying the rulers of Copán, dating from 613; the ball court and hieroglyphic stairway; and the Acropolis, which has superb carved relics of the 16 kings of Copán.

There are hot springs a one-hour drive from the village, and the nearby picturesque mountain village of Santa Rita de Copán has a beautiful plaza and a peaceful colonial church. Don't miss this awesome town, there is so much to do and see and the town itself is splendid.

Tela

Tela is many travelers' favorite Honduran Caribbean beach town. It's a small, quiet place, with superb seafood, several good places to stay and some of the most beautiful beaches on the northern coast. It's basically a place for relaxing and enjoying the simple life. There are plans to boost tourism in the area, so see the place while it's still unspoiled and quiet. The best beach is east of the town, in front of the Hotel Villas Telamar. It has pale, powdery sand and a shady grove of coconut trees.

Trujillo

The small town of Trujillo has played an important role in Central American history. It was near Trujillo on August 14, 1502, that Colombus first set foot on the American mainland. The town sits on the wide arc of the Bahía de Trujillo and is famed for its lovely beaches, coconut palms and gentle seas. Though it has a reputation as one of the country's best Caribbean beach towns, it's not usually full of tourists, except during the annual festival in late June. Apart from the attractions of the beach, there is a 17th-century fortress, the grave of William Walker and a Museo Arqueológico. To the west of the town is the Barrio Cristales, where the Garífuna people live; this is the place to go for music, dancing and revelry.

Bay Islands

Roatán, Guanaja and Utila—50km (31mi) off the north coast of Honduras—are a continuation of the Belizean reefs and offer great snorkeling and diving. The islands' economy is based mostly on fishing, but tourism is becoming increasingly important. Utila retains low-key tourist facilities, while Roatán is gradually joining Guanaja as a more up-market retreat. Most travelers head to West End on Roatán, but Utila is the cheapest of the three islands to visit. Whichever island you visit, make sure you bring plenty of insect repellent, because the sand flies are voracious, especially during the rainy season.

Columbus landed on Guanaja in 1502, but the Spanish later enslaved the islanders and sent them to work on plantations in Cuba and in the gold and silver mines of Mexico. By 1528, the islands were completely depopulated. English, French and Dutch pirates then occupied the islands, followed by the Garífuna, who were shipped here by the British after an uprising on St Vincent. The islands, in many ways, still look more toward England and the US than to the Honduran mainland, and a richly Caribbean version of English is the main language.

Environment

Honduras is the knee of Central America, bordered to the south by Nicaragua and El Salvador and to the west by Guatemala. It has a 644km (399mi) long Caribbean coast and a 124km (77mi) pipsqueak of a Pacific coast. The Caribbean Bay Islands and, further northeast, the distant Swan Islands are both part of Honduran territory.

Three-quarters of the country is composed of rugged hills and mountains, ranging from 300 to nearly 2850m (984 to 9348ft) in height. Lowlands are found only along the coasts and in major river valleys. Deforestation is occurring at a rate of 3000 sq km (1170 sq mi) a year, which, if continued, will turn the country into a treeless desert within the next 20 years. However, there are still largely untouched areas, especially in the Mosquitia region. Fauna includes jaguars, armadillos, wild pigs, monkeys and alligators and abundant bird life such as toucans, herons and kingfishers.

The climate in Honduras varies between the mountainous interior and the coastal lowlands and between the Pacific and Caribbean coasts. The interior is much cooler than the humid coast, and temperate Tegucigalpa has maximum temperatures varying between 25 and 30°C (77 and 86°F).

The rainy season technically begins in May and lasts until October. This means that the interior and Pacific coast are relatively dry between November and April, but on the Caribbean coast it rains all year. The wettest months on the Caribbean coast are from September/October to January/February.

The tourist season on the Caribbean coast is between February and April, during the US winter. This is a good time to visit, but prices will be lower and there will be fewer tourists if you avoid this season.

Chapter
five
Nicaragua

Nicaragua is full of surf. You might want to spend a fair
amount of time exploring the coast. Having a boat can be
super helpful in Nicaragua.

"The best way to cheer yourself up is to cheer somebody else up."
- Mark Twain

Nicaragua is picturesque, from the jagged lava-rock beaches to the gigantic lake in the south that houses the worlds only fresh water sharks. After years of war and internal conflict, present day Nicaraguans simply want to live in peace.

Most Nicaraguans are willing to share their experiences and viewpoints about the conflicts of the past and yet they are eager to move ahead into a more prosperous and cheerful future. Tourism in Nicaragua is less common than in her highly popular neighbor Costa Rica. The natural beauty of Nicaragua is attractive and as the war years fade into memory's dusty shelf, you can expect to see more development and tourism within the country.

This is the largest country in Central America, but you can drive through it rather quickly. Essentially there is only one major highway running through the country and therefore the chances of getting lost are dramatically reduced. There are several police checkpoints along the road. This usually means that two police officers have been dropped off somewhere along the main highway. They stand by the side of the road and wave cars over to conduct their officiating. When pulled over the police ask for your papers and destination and then send you on your way. These procedures seem to be uniform throughout Central America.

Entering Nicaragua

After going through the official Honduran border gate you will pull up to the official Nicaraguan border gate, about 50 yards away. Here the border officials enter your passport number into a book. No charge! Though the officials may request a private donation for their work. You will soon learn that everyone will ask you for money in Nicaragua.

Three Border Crossings

Between Nicaragua and Honduras there are three border crossings; Las Manos (near Ocotal), El Espino (near Somoto), and Guasaule between El Triunfo (Honduras) and Somotillo (Nicaragua).

Aduana and Migration

The Aduana and Migration offices are located another 50 yards down the hill in a semicircular building. When you enter the building several teenagers will request your paperwork. They will show you some official badge which supposedly gives them the right to guide you through the paperwork and to freedom. The officials will search your car and then record all the necessary vehicle information. For example, they will check your vehicle identification number on your engine and record it in your vehicle paperwork. After two hours of confusion and frustration you will leave with the following paperwork and pay the following fees: Certificado de Vehiculos $40 US, Exclusivo Para Moneda Extranjera $20 US and Tarjeta De Turismo $5 US. The second two items must be paid for in US DOLLARS. No exceptions! If you do not have US dollars you will lose money in the exchange with the border exchanger—don't forget to purchase enough money to transit through the country.

Learned Lessons

I'm not sure whether the $40 US I paid for the Certificado de Vehiculos was valid, I think this went into someone's pocket. I asked several officials and never got a straight answer. Be prepared, these are the games that border officials like to play. I was also solicited several times for propina by a number of the officials at the Nicaraguan entry point. I was suspicious about the $40 US fee and keep referring to this payment and therefore I was never coerced into paying anything additional.

Special Directions

Bring US currency for your entry into Nicaragua, $35 US. Also check your forms for proper entry and exit dates. If you plan on staying for more than 3 days you can request a 30 day permit for your vehicle and person. There is no additional cost for the thirty day permit.

The police treat tourists differently than they treat people solely in transit and if you decide to stay for more than three days you won't have to deal with extending your visa.

Nicaraguan Border/Managua

DRIVING TIME: 3 hour

KILOMETERS: 200

MILES: 121

HWY: CA 1

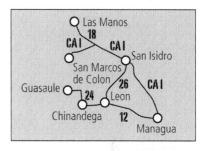

The roads in Nicaragua are the worst of any in all of Central America. As mentioned above, it is difficult to get lost because CA 1 is really the only major road running through the country. Follow the signs to Managua, if you find any.

Depending on how long the border entry and exit procedures take, you can make it through Nicaragua in one day. Most likely you will be given a transit visa good for 3 days. My recommendation is to travel on to San Juan del Sur and spend a day or two in this incredible town and then cross the border into Costa Rica. San Juan del Sur is only 45 minutes from the Costa Rican border; it is truly a fantastic place!

Learned Lessons

The officials at the border will ask you what your final destination is for the day, then they will indicate it on your Tarjeta De Turismo.

This is not your final destination for the trip through Nicaragua, it is your destination for the day that you enter Nicaragua. Regardless of where you are going, tell them Penas Blancas at the Costa Rican border. I told the officer at the Honduran-Nicaraguan border that I was traveling to Managua that day. Thus Managua was written as my final destination for the day of entry on my Tarjeta De Turismo. When I was stopped about one hour north of San Juan del Sur, the officer told me that I must go back to Managua and receive permission to travel past Managua that day.

After some discussion and a small donation, I was allowed to proceed. Check your paperwork before you leave the Nicaraguan border and make sure that the officer writes down the city that you indicate. Games, games and more games!

Special Directions

Driving away from the Honduran border you will encounter little civilization. There are few places to eat until you arrive to Managua, thus fill your stomach and tanks near the border. But don't eat too much because the roads leading to Managua are horrible, be prepared for a rough ride.

Managua/San Juan del Sur

DRIVING TIME: 3 hours
KILOMETERS: 141
MILES: 88
HWY: CA 1—CA 2

When entering Managua stay on the straight-away and follow the signs to Central. About 10 minutes after entering the city you will come across a sign that reads Jinotepe CA 2. Steer left, this is the road you want. Follow this road until you meet with a traffic circle. Follow the traffic circle around and exit UNI-UNAN.

There is a large sign, you can't miss it. This road will eventually lead out of town and on to the road for Penas Blancas and San Juan del Sur.

* Please note that the Interamerican Hwy changes from CA 1 to CA 2 until the border with Costa Rica.

The exit for San Juan del Sur is about 10 minutes past Rivas. From the main road it's another 18K to the coastal town. Follow the road all the way to the beach. If you have come this far, please don't miss San Juan del Sur, it's one of the most beautiful places along the entire trip. Take a hike along the coast in either direction, there are some fabulous tidal pools. There is also some decent surf at the river mouth, just ask the locals. There are several surf camps to the north and south, ask the locals in town and get ready to score some epic waves.

Hotel & Eats

Casa Internacional Joxi is a half block from the beach and has great service and food. John, the Norwegian owner, offers fax, telephone and Internet services to his guests. He has rooms with air conditioning and private baths for $15 US. This town offers great seafood, a large lobster dinner will cost you about $7 US. There are several restaurants located on the beach, enjoy yourself! The people are eager to speak of their experiences and they are very friendly.

The Costa Rican border is 24k past Rivas. The road is horrible, it takes about one hour to reach the border from Rivas or San Juan del Sur.

Learned Lessons

In Managua at the traffic circle follow the signs to UNI -UNAN. The signs do not indicate Jinotape CA 2 anywhere. This is a puzzling spot so make sure you make the correct turn-off.

Special Directions

For some peculiar reason CA 1 becomes CA 2 between Managua and the Costa Rican border. Again, it's always better to use cities as references, the road signs and road numbers mean very little to the local people.

Exiting Nicaragua

DRIVING TIME: 1 hours
KILOMETERS: 24
MILES: 88
HWY: CA 1—CA 2

If you thought entering Nicaragua was difficult, you are in for a surprise because exiting is even more of a headache. Again you will need a guide. Any of the teen-agers will do, cost for a guide will run about $6 US. There are various stops you need to make. One with Migration $1 US, one with the transit police $2 US, and one with the Aduana.

The Aduana official will request your paperwork and then send you down the road for copies of your passport, car title and driver's license. Once all the copies are delivered and the official finishes recording, stamping and officiating, you are on your way. Show you paperwork to the guards at the exit gate and proceed to the

Costa Rican border entry 4k down the road.

The Costa Rican border is 24k past Rivas. The road is horrible, it takes about one hour to reach the border from Rivas or San Juan del Sur.

Learned Lessons
These exit procedures take about 1-2 hours. Plan accordingly, you need time to process your paperwork on the Costa Rican side. The roads leading to and away from the border are very bad, so drive carefully.

Exchange your money on the Costa Rican side, the rates are better. It is also helpful to have extra copies of your passport, car title and driver's license—the officials will ask for them when you exit Nicaragua.

Special Directions
You will be approached by several kids that will want to watch your car. Pick one and let him know he is responsible, $1 US.

Enjoying Nicaragua

Managua
The capital of Nicaragua is spread across the southern shore of Lago de Managua and is crowded with more than a quarter of Nicaragua's population. It's been racked by natural disasters, including two earthquakes this century, and since the 1972 earthquake the city has had no center. Those returning to Managua after a few years will notice marked changes. An improving economy has produced a construction boom. It will be obvious, however, that the recovering economy has not benefited everyone, as poverty is still widespread.

Several of Managua's attractions stand around the Plaza de la República, including the lakeside municipal cathedral, which has been reconditioned with help from foreign donors and is now open to the public. Near the cathedral is the recently renovated Palacio Nacional, which has two giant paintings of Augusto Sandino and Carlos Fonseca at the entrance.

The Huellas de Acahualinca museum houses the ancient footprints of people and animals running toward the lake from a volcanic eruption. The Museo de la Revolución has interesting historical exhibits with an emphasis on the revolutionary struggle of this century. There are also several lagunas, or volcanic crater lakes, which are popular swimming spots.

Barrio Martha Quezada is a residential district with many simple, cheap guesthouses and places to eat. This is where backpackers tend to congregate. On weekends there's dancing and partying around Plaza 19 de Julio.

Around Managua

The large volcano at the center of Parque Nacional Volcán Masaya National Park , which still steams and belches, is surrounded by smaller volcanoes and thermal springs. Legends say that the Indians used to throw young women into the boiling lava to appease Chaciutique, the goddess of fire. The Spanish believed it was the entrance to hell, inhabited by devils. Entrance to the park is only 14 miles (23km) southeast of Managua. The Laguna de Xiloá, a stunning crater lake 12 miles (20km) northwest of the city, is a favorite swimming spot. At El Trapiche, 11 miles (17km) southeast of the city, water from natural springs has been channeled into large outdoor pools surrounded by gardens and restaurants.

León

León is traditionally the most liberal of Nicaragua's cities and remains the radical and intellectual center of the country. Monuments to the revolution, including bold Sandinista murals, are dotted all over town, and many buildings are riddled with bullet holes. Though scarred by earthquakes and war, the city is resplendent with many fine colonial churches and official buildings. Its streets are lined with old Spanish-style houses that have white adobe walls, red-tiled roofs, thick wooden doors and cool garden patios. Its cathedral is the largest in Central America and features huge paintings of the Stations of the Cross by Antonio Sarria as well as the tomb of poet Rubén Darío. The Galería de Héroes y Mártires has a display that includes photos of those who died fighting for the FSLN during the 1978-79 revolution.

The Caribbean Coast

Unlike the rest of Nicaragua, the Caribbean coast was never colonized: It remained a British protectorate until the late 1800s. The only part of the rain forest-covered coast usually visited by travelers is Bluefields, but some visitors also head out to the Corn Islands (Islas del Maíz). The journey from Managua to Bluefields involves a five-hour boat trip down the Río Escondido. Bluefields' mix of ethnic groups— including Indians (Miskitos, Ramas and Sumos), blacks and mestizos from the rest of Nicaragua—makes it an interesting place, and the people here definitely like to have a good time; there are several reggae clubs and plenty of dancing on the weekends.

Granada

Granada, nicknamed 'La Gran Sultana' is reference to its Moorish namesake in Spain, is Nicaragua's oldest Spanish city. Founded in 1524 by conquistadores, it rumps up against the imposing Volcán Mombacho on the the northwest shore of Lake Nicaragua. With its access to the Caribbean Sea via the lake and the San Juan River, Granada has always been a main trade center. Today the town is relatively quiet and a major literary center, and retains its colonial character. It's a wonderful walking city, with most major attractions, including the Cathedral and Parque Colón, within a few blocks of the plaza. When you're ready to cool off, the lake is only a 15-minute walk away. The Assumption of Mary (August 15) is the town's biggest party day.

Nicaragua Environment

Nicaragua is the largest country in Central America. It's bordered to the north by Honduras, to the south by Costa Rica, to the east by the Caribbean Sea and to the west by the Pacific Ocean. The country has three distinct geographic regions: the Pacific lowlands, the north-central mountains and the Caribbean lowlands, also called the Mosquito Coast or Mosquitía. The fertile Pacific lowlands are interrupted by about 40 volcanoes, and dominated by Lago de Nicaragua, which is the largest lake in Central America. The Mosquito Coast is a sparsely populated rain forest area and the outlet for many of the large rivers originating in the central mountains. To date, 17% of the country has been given national-park status.

Lago de Nicaragua supports unusual fish, including the world's only freshwater sharks, as well as a huge variety of bird life. The cloud- and rain forest in the northwest contain abundant wildlife including ocelots, warthogs, pumas, jaguars, sloths and spider monkeys. Avian life in the forests is particularly rich: The cinnamon hummingbird, ruddy woodpecker, stripe-breasted wren, elegant trogon, shining hawk and even the quetzal, the holy bird of the Maya, can all be seen. The jungles on the Caribbean coast contain trees that grow up to almost 200ft (60m) high and are home to boas, anacondas, jaguars, deer and howler monkeys.

Nicaragua's climate varies according to altitude. The Pacific lowlands are always extremely hot, but the air is fresh and the countryside green during the rainy season (May to November); the dry season (December to April) brings winds that send clouds of brown dust across the plains. The Caribbean coast is hot and wet; it can rain heavily even during the brief dry season (March to May). The mountains of the north are much cooler than the lowlands.

Nicaragua was devastated by Hurricane Mitch in November 1998, when more than a year's worth of rain fell in in just seven days. A series of violent earthquakes and volcanic eruptions in the fall of 1999 didn't help the situation much.

Special Surf Section

Nicargaua is a swell magnet for South swells, a long season spanning approximately nine months from March to November. Deepwater swell averages 3-5 ft with bigger swells of 6-8ft occuring regularly especially from April-October. Due to the Lago de Nicaragua effect, the wind blows offshore all year. With solid South swells and some of the best points, rock reefs and sandbars in Central America this is a recipe for perfection. Unlike Costa Rica to the south, Nicaragua's best surf breaks are not spread out all over the country but concentrated in one area along its SW Pacific coastline in the province of Rivas. Most of the surf is hard to find, difficult to access and requires a 4x4 truck or a boat.

Popular Surf Lodge

POPOYO SURF LODGE is located in Las Salinas, in Nicaragua's Rivas Province, 2.5 hrs. from Managua, hosted by expatriate Floridian surfer JJ Yemma and his staff which includes resident surf guides John, Mike and Manuel. Popoyo guests will be met at the international airport in Managua by Popoyo staff and transferred directly to Popoyo Surf Resort and do not need to rent a vehicle. Base package includes 6 nights/7 days accomodation, 3 meals per day, all non-alcoholic beverages and daily surf tours. There is a cash bar which sells cold beers and mixed drinks. Popoyo's hardware now includes 2 boats, a 25ft boat with a soft roof and 85hp Yamaha outboard, and a new 26ft boat with a hard roof and 150hp Yamaha outboard. Both boats shown here are fully outfitted for surfing and near shore fishing. See www.wavehunters.com for more info.

Top Five Google Search For 'Nicaragua'

http://travel.state.gov/travel/cis_pa_tw/cis/cis_985.html
http://www.state.gov/r/pa/ei/bgn/1850.htm
http://en.wikipedia.org/wiki/Nicaragua
http://news.bbc.co.uk/2/hi/americas/country_profiles/1225218.stm
http://www.lonelyplanet.com/nicaragua

Top Three Google Search 'Drive To Nicaragua'

http://www.nicaliving.com/node/11838
http://www.travelblog.org/Central-America-Caribbean/Nicaragua/Southern-Pacific-Coast/San-Juan-del-Sur/blog-336645.html
http://www.nicamigo.com/travel_nica.html

Chapter
six
Costa Rica

One of my favorite shot. We were on our way to Arenal and
it started erupting, the ground was shaking and I grabbed
my camera and took this shot before the clouds covered up
the entire mountain.

*"I think the next best thing to solving a problem
is finding some humor in it."
- Frank Howard Clark*

Costa Rica is fascinating and beautiful; there are tropical rain forests, active volcanoes, and white sand beaches that stretch as far as the imagination. The country is by far the most developed of all Central American countries. There are presently over hundreds of thousands North-Americans living in Costa Rica and the number is growing daily.

Both Caribbean and Pacific coasts offer beautiful beaches, national parks and festive environments. There have been recent increases in taxes and therefore it is more expensive to travel in Costa Rica than the other Central American countries. But compared to North American standards, food and accommodations are still a bargain.

Tourism is booming in Costa Rica, just walk into any bookstore and you will find an assortment of travel guides containing information on retiring, moving, investing, living, rafting, bungee jumping or whatever you want to do in the country. People are willing to pay to have fun and this has been well-displayed by the expanding list of activities that tourists may enjoy while visiting Costa Rica. Unfortunately, you won't find the peace and solitude that was so attractive years ago when the spines of tourism had not yet scratched the skin of Costa Rica. Nevertheless, it's still a wonderful country to visit and it is my favorite in all of Central America.

Surfing, Water Sports & Stoke

Surfers, welcome to paradise! Costa Rica offers beach breaks, reef breaks and off shore islands with a plethora of waves. Eight hours from coast to coast—two separate oceans within one day's drive—substantially increases your odds of locating surf. I have been to CR thirteen times in that last twenty years and it never ceases to amaze me—yes, it's much different now but it still has a charm and character that is timeless, the people are fantastic and the beaches are boundless. Costa Rica is a paradise worth exploring and an experience worth having—however you get there, just do it!

Driving In Costa Rica

Watch your speed in Costa Rica, the police like to catch foreigners in radar traps. Also, there is a seat-belt law—so wear it! The roads are horrible but the signs are good. From the border you can make San Jose in 5 hours. From San Jose you can visit either coast in a couple of hours.

One Entry Point

Penas Blancas is the only entry point for Costa Rica. There are no vehicle entry points on the Caribbean side coming from Nicaragua. Therefore you must travel past Managua and south toward the Pacific coast into Costa Rica.

Fumigation

Your first stop is fumigation, a few $ US. Pay the fee and then drive your car through the fumigation station. If you are adamantly against having your car fumigated, you can offer the inspector some extra dinero and they will most likely give you passage without fumigation.

Migration & Aduana

The Costa Rican and Nicaraguan immigration offices are 4km apart. On the Costa Rican side the immigration office is next to the Restaurant La Frontera.

Your next stop is the Migration and Aduana, both in one building—what a concept! Park your vehicle and go to Migration for your entry stamp, a few more $ US. Next take your passport and title and give it to the official at the Aduana window.

You are required to purchase insurance for a minimum of one month, about $30 US. The official will give you four forms, computer generated: Certificado De Entrega De Vehiculos, No Comerciales Importacion Temporal, Instituto Nacional De Seguros, and Recibo De Dinero.

After you receive the forms you are free to go. There is an inspection station at the exit about 1k down the road, but it is very informal.

Learned Lessons

You will encounter several checkpoints on the road leading away from the border. The guards will ask for your passport and destination and then send you on your way with a smile. These stations are more for illegal immigrants from Nicaragua than for gringos.

Special Directions

This is by far the most efficient and trustworthy crossing you will encounter. If you have made it this far, congratulations!

CR Border/Tamarindo

DRIVING TIME: 4 hours

KILOMETERS: 162

MILES: 100

HWY: CA 1-CA 151-CA 21-CA 152

As mentioned above, you will come across several checkpoints traveling away from the Nicaraguan border. Show the officials the necessary paperwork and you should have no problems.

From Penas Blancas follow the signs to Liberia. At Liberia you can fill your gas tank and stomach before continuing to Tamarindo. In the center of town turn right at the major intersection and follow the signs to Tamarindo. This same route will take you to Coco Beach, Playa Junquillal, Samara, Nicoya or any other location on the Nicoya Peninsula.

There are several exceptional National Parks in this region. If you see only one National Park while in Costa Rica, make it Santa Rosa National Park. The park is located between Penas Blancas and Liberia about 45 minutes from the border and 35k north of Liberia. The beach is unimaginably beautiful, there is an abundance of wildlife in the park and there are camping facilities and cabanas for rent. There is also a cooking facility that provides meals for a small fee. There are three alternative routes leaving Tamarindo for locations further south. Depending on how far on to the Nicoya Peninsula you have traveled, you may either (1) work your way back to Liberia and continue south from the city, (2) take the short ferry at the northern Golfo de Nicoya, or (3) travel by ferry at the southern end of the Nicoya Peninsula to Puntarenas.

Learned Lessons

If you're well on to the Nicoya Peninsula you may want to take the ferry. This can sometimes take much longer than anticipated. The ferry operator will wait until the ferry is full before leaving the port and there is frequently a long line of cars waiting to cross—ordinarily more than can fit on the ferry, so get there early.

Special Directions

The ferry that sails from the Nicoya Peninsula to Puntarenus departs from Playa Naranjo. There are three to five daily departures and the travel takes between 1 to 2 hours. The cost is between $8 and $10 for you and your wheels. Check departure times by calling Conatramar at 661-1069.

CR Border / San Jose

DRIVING TIME: 5 hours
KILOMETERS: 289
MILES: 179
HWY: CA 1

After finishing your entry requirements follow the signs on CA 1 to Liberia. From Liberia continue south 128k to Esparza. At Esparza head for San Mateo. San Mateo is the junction point for San Jose or the Pacific coast.

Follow the signs toward Alajuela and San Jose. This road leads you away from San Mateo and up into the highlands, the road is well-marked, but the ascent is steep. When you are close to San Jose you will pass the airport, about 15 minutes from town. Plan your drive into San Jose on a weekday and not during the rush hour, the traffic can be horrific. Like all Latin American capitals, driving in San Jose is not for the weak or impatient. The roads are congested and confusing, expect to pull over several times to ask for directions. Attendants at gas stations are always helpful, nonetheless, be prepared to take your time finding the way.

Hotel & Eats

If you have been driving for some time and want a great place to lay your tired bones, try Hotel Cacts. As you enter San Jose on Paseo Colon you will pass Pizza Hut. Turn right at the next corner and travel 4 blocks to Hotel Cacts. The cost is $25—$50 per night, it includes a hot shower and a light breakfast. They have 24 hour security for your car, a travel agency on-site and storage for your luggage. When you pass the Pizza Hut, turn left and drive 4 blocks.

Learned Lessons

Watch your personal items in the coastal towns and in San Jose. Never leave anything of value in your vehicle unattended. There are plenty of car parks in San Jose, but don't trust them and never leave your keys with them. Read Helpful Hints & Other Topics for more information.

Special Directions

San Mateo is the junction point for San Jose or the Pacific coast.

San Jose

San José, pronounced is the capital and largest city of Costa Rica. Located in the Central Valley, San José is the seat of national government, the focal point of political and economic activity, and the major transportation hub of this Central American nation. Founded in 1738 by order of Cabildo de León, San José is one of the youngest capital cities in Latin America by year of conception, though it was not named capital until 1823. Today it is a modern city with bustling commerce, brisk expressions of art and architecture, and spurred by the country's improved tourism industry, it is a significant destination and stopover for foreign visitors.

The population of San José Canton is 365,799 though the metropolitan area stretches beyond the canton limits and comprises a third of the country's population. San José exerts a strong influence on a wider range because of its proximity to minor cities (Alajuela, Heredia and Cartago) and the country's demographic assemblage in the Central Valley. The city lies at a mean elevation of 1,161 m above sea level, and enjoys a stable climate throughout the year, with an average temperature of 25oC (77oF) and annual precipitation of 1800 mm, more than 90% of it falling in the rainy season from May to November

Pacific Coast

FROM CR BORDER

DRIVING TIME: 5 hours

KILOMETERS: 289

MILES: 179

Those traveling to the Pacific coast must turn right at the junction point of San Mateo and head for Jaco. The three main travel destinations on this route are Jaco, Quepos and Dominical. All three locations are worth a visit. You can also drive to the Panamanian border via this route, but the roads are worse.

The road from Jaco to Dominical takes a toll on your vehicle and spine. Jaco is your first coastal town within striking distance of San Jose. This is where all the Ticos go for vacation and weekend holidays, thus be prepared for crowds. Playa de Jaco is a great place to relax during the week, but on the weekends the ambiance changes to a festival of loud discos and, at times, a drunken calamity. This is a large coastal town with all the amenities of any resort location. Quepos is a much quieter town then Jaco. It is located about 1+ hours south of Jaco and it is the home of Manuel Antonio, a great National Park worth the entry fee. Another 1-2 hours south is Dominical, a small coastal town with a great atmosphere. If you are a surfer you will definitely want to check out this place, even when there is no swell it's thumping.

If you are looking to get away from the tourists and into the outskirts of Costa Rica keep heading south toward Golfito and the Panamanian border. From Dominical it's another 6 hour drive. Head for San Isidro, and then south toward Golfito, 190K. Again for those surfing enthusiasts there is a great break at Pavones. If you're in Dominical and a swell comes in, pack the camping gear and head for

Pavones and some long left-handers, check out http://www.pavonescostarica.com for more information. The drive from Golfito is about 1.5 hours over a dirt road or you can fly from San Jose for $100 on flysansa.com

Traveling during the rainy season the road to the south of Dominical may not be passable, ask the local Ticos for road conditions before you make the long trek.

Learned Lessons
If your driving past Jaco make sure your spare is in working order. These are some of the worst roads you will encounter in Costa Rica. The roads are passable, but they are muddy and filled with potholes during the rainy season.

Special Directions
After finishing your entry requirements follow the signs on CA 1 to Liberia. From Liberia continue south 128k to Esparza. At Esparza head for San Mateo. San Mateo is the junction point for San Jose or the Pacific coast.

Driving Around San Jose
One must be very patient driving in San Jose and around the city. There are radar traps on most roads and in many instances the police will pull you over and ask to see your papers, passport, and drivers license. In most cases, unless you were speeding, the police will simply check your documents and let you go on your way.

The city center is arranged on a grid, avenidas run east-west and calles north-south. Street numbers are rarely given in San Jose, instead, the nearest intersection is given. Thus you can assume that the directions to any particular local are not exact, but at least in the general vicinity.

The downtown area is dirty and congested, parking is difficult and vehicle break-ins are common. Find a safe place to park your vehicle and pay to have it watched.

There are plenty of places to stay, though the better B&Bs tend to be booked well in advance, thus if you have a particular place in mind it is wise to call ahead and reserve a room.

Special Directions

The population of the city itself is about a third of a million, the province ups the total to 1.2 million, approximately 40% of the countries population.

San Jose/Caribbean

DRIVING TIME: 4 hours

KILOMETERS: 134

MILES: 83 Hwy: CA 1—CA 2

This is a beautiful drive through mountains (you actually go through a mountain), banana and mango plantations and lush tropical forests. The major problem is finding your way through San Jose and to the Caribbean route. You want to follow any sign you see for Limon. Travel north, up Avenida Central to the traffic circle in the center of town. At the traffic circle follow the road around to the left. This road takes you to the junction point where the road for Limon is located. Be prepared to ask for directions.

Learned Lessons

Once you are in Limon—get out of Limon! This is not why you came to the Caribbean. There is a traffic signal, the third when you enter town, with a fruit stand on the corner. You want to turn right at the corner and travel south toward Cahuita and Puerto Viejo.

Cahuita National Park is located at the northern end of Cahuita. There is a trail that follows the cost for several kilometers and empties on to a deserted palm lined beach. Along the trail you may encounter monkeys, sloths and giant mosquitoes—don't forget your repellent!

Cahuita is about one hour from Limon and Puerto Viejo is another 45 minutes south of Cahuita. Puerto Viejo offers great surfing (Salsa Brava) and festive night life at inexpensive prices. Those going to Puerto Viejo from Cahuita must travel back to the main road and turn left at the junction. Be prepared for a bumpy ride!

Special Directions

Take precaution while traveling these roads. Watch your speed and make sure your vehicle papers are in order. The police always set up checkpoints in this region. You are close to Panama and you will most likely be solicited by drug dealers in the coastal towns. Be cautious and don't forget that you're in a foreign country, drug offenders are not treated nicely by authorities.

San Jose/Panama Border

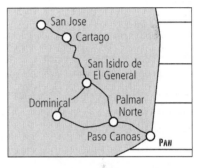

DRIVING TIME: 8 hours
KILOMETERS: 355
MILES: 220
HWY: CA 2

This is a long drive over the mountains into the lowlands of Costa Rica. Leaving San Jose head for Cartago, CA 2. Once in Cartago, go through the town and the road will veer right. There are no signs, so you may have to stop and ask.

After you leave the city you will ascend into the mountains again. This is a demanding drive with twists, turns, and potholes.

Eventually you will reach San Isidro in 3 to 4 hours. From San Isidro you may visit Dominical on the coast or continue south toward Golfito and the Panamanian border. Leaving San Isidro, head for Palmar Norte and then continue on to Paso Canoas or Golfito.

Paso Canoas is the main border crossing between Panama and Costa Rica. The border is open from 6:00 a.m.-11:00 a.m. and from 1:00 p.m.-10:00 p.m. Check with the consulate in San Jose for current requirements for Panama visa requirements.

Travelers note that the Interamerican Hwy changes from CA 1 to CA 2 past Cartago to the border with Panama.

Learned Lessons

If you're driving into Panama with the intention of traveling to South America there is an obstacle called the Darien Gap. This mass of tropical jungle prevents anyone from driving between Central and South American. There is a ferry boat from Colon, Panama to Caragena, Colombia.

Crossing the Darien Gap

You don't actually cross the Darien Gap, you go around it by boat. The crossing is made on a small cruise ship that takes about 17 hours. See the special section in the last chapter for more info.

Special Directions

If you visit the south and you are returning to northern Costa Rica you may drive up the coast from Dominical or through the central route. From Dominical you may continue north to Quepos and Jaco and then on to San Jose. Check with the locals before you make the trip about the condition of the road.

Exiting Costa Rica

No special permit is required if you haven't overstayed the time allocated in your passport. If your time has expired, you will need an exit visa which you can pay for at the border. When you enter Panama from Costa Rica make sure that your papers indicate that you will be leaving Panama from Colon and not the border post in which you have entered. Incorrect papers can cause grief. Insurance for your vehicle is available near the border at $70 for 90 days.

Costa Rica & Nicaragua: Penas Blancas is the main border post between Costa Rica and Nicaragua. The border is open from 8am until 8pm daily. The Costa Rican and Nicaraguan border stations are 4km apart.

Costa Rica & Panama: There are three main border crossings between Costa Rica and Panama. The most frequented crossing is at Paso Canoas; open from 6am until 9pm. Officials may require an onward ticket and proof of sufficient funds. The closest city of any size is David, about one hour from the border. From Da vid, Panama City is another 6-7 hours travel. On the Caribbean side you may cross into Panama at Sixaola, open from 7am until 7pm.

The last crossing point is at Rio Sereno, east from San Vito, this is a remote and rarely used route and the border officials are known to be sticklers on regulations and formalities.

Special Directions
The one major crossing between Costa Rica and Nicaragua is Penas Blancas, on the Carretera Interamericana.

Parque Nacional Volcán Arenal

At the center of a national park in the northwest of the country, the perfectly conical, 1633m (5356ft) Volcán Arenal is everyone's image of a typical volcano. The volcano has been exceptionally active since 1968, when huge explosions triggered lava flows that killed several dozen people.

The degree of activity varies from week to week; sometimes there is a spectacular display of flowing red-hot lava and incandescent rocks flying through the air; at other times, the volcano is more placid and gently glows in the dark. Don't even think about climbing Arenal. The best views at night (when the weather is clear) are from the western or northern side.

Parque Nacional Santa Rosa

This is the oldest and one of the best developed national parks in Costa Rica. It covers most of the Península Santa Elena, which juts out into the Pacific in the far northwestern corner of the country. It protects the largest remaining stand of tropical dry forest in CentralAmerica and important nesting sites for endangered species of sea turtle. The park also has historical connections, and includes the hacienda where an amateur Costa Rican army took on William Walker in 1856.

Monteverde

This small community in northwestern Costa Rica was founded by Quakers in 1951 and is now a popular and interesting destination for both local and international visitors. Its attractions include a cloud forest, walking trails, quetzals, a cheese factory, a butterfly garden and a number of art galleries.

Caribbean Coast

The Caribbean has more cultural diversity than the Pacific coast. Half of this coastal area is protected by national parks and wildlife refuges, which has slowed development and the building of access roads, making it an especially verdant place to get away from it all. The main city is Puerto Limón, which has a tropical park teeming with flowers and sloths. Parque Nacional Tortuguero is the most important Caribbean breeding ground of the green sea turtle and has plenty of birds, monkeys and lizards. The Creole beach paradise of Cahuita has a nearby national park with attractive beaches, coral reef and coastal rain forest. Bribri culture can be experienced in the surfing mecca of Puerto Viejo de Talamanca. Handicrafts, reggae, home stays and cultural tours make Puerto Viejo an especially interesting destination.

Península de Nicoya

This area on the northwestern Pacific coast is difficult to traverse because of the lack of paved roads; however, it's well worth the effort because it contains some of the country's best and most remote beaches. There are also some small and rarely visited wildlife reserves and parks. Parque Nacional Marino las Baulas de Guanacaste, just north of Tamarindo, includes Playa Grande, an important nesting site for the baula (leatherback turtle)—the world's largest turtle, which can weigh over 500kg (1105lb). Playa del Coco is the most accessible beach on the peninsula, in an attractive setting and with a small village, which has some nightlife. Good surfing and windsurfing can be found at Playa Tamarindo. Caving fans head for Parque Nacional Barra Honda, northeast of Nicoya, which protects some of Costa Rica's most interesting caves. Wildlife teems in the coastal Refugio Nacional de Fauna Silvestre Ostional, midway between Sámara and Paraíso. The main attraction is the annual nesting of the olive ridley sea turtle, but you'll also find iguanas, howler monkeys, coatimundis and flocks of numerous birds. One of the safest and prettiest beaches in the country is Playa Sámara, and Montezuma, near the tip of the peninsula, is a lovely, laid-back paradise for tired, young gringos.

Surf Along The Way

Driving along the pacific coast of Mexico one will find never-ending stretches of uninhabited beach full of epic surf. El Salvador, Nicaragua, Costa Rica, and Panama all have popular, well-known breaks—it's the unknown breaks that will fill your excite meter on this road trip.

Costa Rica already has quite a reputation among surfers, who are drawn there from near and far by the quality and consistency of its waves. Though the country gets plenty of the big waves that true surf fanatics live for, there are also days and spots that are perfect for people who have little experience with the sport, or who have been away from the ocean for a long time, and would like to try it again. This means that whether you're a veteran wave ripper or a belly-boarding beginner, you can usually find the conditions you need to have a great time.

With 755 miles of coastline on two oceans, Costa Rica has more breaks than you can shake a stick at. The country's selection of surf spots range from idyllic beach breaks to coral platforms where the water leaps up and tubes like a miniature Pipeline. Having coastline on two oceans is quite an advantage, since when one ocean is flat, there is usually something breaking on the other side of the country. Often enough, there is good surf pumping on both coasts.

And the country's surf is complemented by its comfortable water temperatures -- you can leave that wet suit at home -- beautiful scenery, and the convenience of a variety of accommodations and restaurants near most breaks. Since it is five times longer than the Caribbean coast, the Pacific has considerably more surfing spots. Many of the country's best breaks are found in the northwest province of Guanacaste, but there are also some excellent spots in the Central Pacific and Southern Zones. And the few breaks that are available in the Caribbean province of Limon are certainly nothing to complain about.

The following is a listing of the country's best surf spots: Pacific Guanacaste Potrero Grande: Right point break in Santa Rosa National Park, only accessible by boat; no camping. Playa Naranjo: Great beach break by Witch's Rock, in Santa Rosa National Park, accessible with four-wheel-drive vehicle or boat; camping permitted. Playa Grande: Very consistent beach break north of Tamarindo.

Tamarindo: Good beach break, excellent base for surfing nearby beaches.
Playa Langosta: River mouth break south of Tamarindo.
Avellanas: Very good beach break further to the south.
Playa Negra: Right point break further to the south.
Nosara: Several beach breaks near selection of accommodations.
Central Boca Barranca: Long river mouth left just south of Puntarenas.
Tivives: Beach breaks and river-mouth left, south of Puntarenas.
Jaco: Popular beach break with abundance of hotels and restaurants.
Hermosa: Several very consistent beach breaks south of Jaco.
Manuel Antonio: Beach breaks near plentiful accommodations.
Dominical: Great beach breaks near hotels and restaurants.
Matapalo: Right point break at tip of Osa Peninsula.
Pavones: Very long left at mouth of Golfo Dulce.
Carribean Playa Bonita: Left over reef off popular beach just north of Limon City.
Cahuita: Beach break on Black Beach, near hotels and restaurants.
Puerto Viejo: Fast right over coral reef, plenty of hotels and restaurants.
Cocles: Beach break just south of Puerto Viejo.
Manzanillo: Beach break, only when big, some accommodations nearby.
Costa Rica Activities

Costa Rica's national parks offer a huge variety of hiking—the following are just two of the highlights. The Parque Nacional Rincón de la Vieja, northeast of Liberia in northwestern Costa Rica, is a volcanic wonderland of cones, craters, lagoons, boiling mud pools and sulphur springs. The park can be explored on foot or horseback, and visitors can bathe in the hot springs. There are long-distance hiking trails in the Parque Nacional Corcovado, which is in the southwestern corner of the Península de Osa in the south of the country. The trails offer visitors the chance to spend several days walking through lowland tropical rain forest. Make sure you visit in the dry season, and keep your eyes peeled for wildlife. There are shorter walks around Monteverde and in the coastal Parque Nacional Manuel Antonio, south of Quepos.

Bird watchers should head to the rain forests at La Selva (in the central north) and to the Parque Nacional Tapantí (southeast of Cartago), Parque Nacional Palo Verde (at the head of the Golfo de Nicoya), Refugio Nacional de Vida Silvestre Caño Negro (east of Upala) and the area around Tortuguero. Turtle watchers should visit Parque Nacional Tortuguero, where they can visit nesting sites and watch the turtles lay their eggs. There are also turtles at Parque Nacional Santa Rosa. Different species of turtle lay their eggs at different times of the year; check your biology textbooks for details.

Pavones on the Pacific Coast reportedly has some of the best surfing in Central America. There is also good surfing at Playa Naranjo in northwestern Costa Rica and at Puerto Viejo on the Caribbean coast. Windsurfers should check out the artificial Laguna de Arenal, near the spectacular volcano. There are snorkeling and diving possibilities at the Reserva Biologica Isla del Cano, 20km (12mi) west of Bahía Drake, off the northern part of the Península de Nicoya and in the Parque Nacional Isla del Coco—an isolated island 500km (310mi) southwest of Costa Rica in the eastern Pacific.

Golfito is a center for deep-sea fishing, and there are plenty of opportunities to charter boats for several days or more. Parsimina, a small village at the mouth of the Río Parsimina, 50km (31mi) northwest of Limón, has several excellent fishing lodges and good offshore reef fishing.

Río Reventazon, in central Costa Rica, is one of the most exciting and scenic rivers in Costa Rica and a favorite with river rafters and kayakers. The river is navigable year-round, but June and July are the best months. Río Pacure, the next major river valley east, is perhaps even more scenic and offers the best white-water rafting in the country through spectacular canyons clothed in virgin rain forest. Turrialba is the best base for these excursions.

Costa Rica Environment
Costa Rica is bordered to the north by Nicaragua and to the east by Panama. It has both a Caribbean and a Pacific coast. A series of volcanic mountain chains runs

from the Nicaraguan border in the northwest to the Panamanian border in the southeast, splitting the country in two. In the center of these ranges is a high-altitude plain, with coastal lowlands on either side. Over half the population lives on this plain, which has fertile volcanic soils. The Caribbean coast is 212km (131mi) long and is characterized by mangroves, swamps and sandy beaches. The Pacific coast is much more rugged and rocky, and, thanks to a number of gulfs and peninsulas, is a tortuous 1016km (630mi) long.

The country's biodiversity attracts nature lovers from all over the world. The primary attraction for many visitors is the 850 recorded bird species, which include the resplendent quetzal, indigo-capped hummingbirds, macaws and toucans. Costa Rica's tropical forests have over 1400 tree species and provide a variety of habitats for the country's fauna including four types of monkey, sloths, armadillos, jaguars and tapirs. There are also a number of dazzling butterflies. National parks cover almost 12% of the country, and forest reserves and Indian reservations boost the protected land area to 27%.

Costa Rica is a tropical country and experiences only two seasons: wet and dry. The dry season is generally between late December and April, and the wet season lasts the rest of the year. The Caribbean coast tends to be wet all year. Temperatures vary little between seasons; the main influence on temperature is altitude. San José at 1150m (3772ft) has a climate that the locals refer to as 'eternal Spring': lows average 15°C (60°F); highs average 26°C (79°F). The coasts are much hotter, with the Caribbean averaging 21°C (70°F) at night and over 30°C (86°F) during the day; the Pacific is a few degrees warmer still. The humidity at low altitudes can be oppressive.

Costa Rica/Traffic Tickets

There is a good chance that you will be stopped at some point by the police in Costa Rica. Make sure that your paperwork is order and that your visa and car insurance are current. If not you could lose your vehicle or vehicle plates to the police. If you get pulled over for speeding or some other infraction you will be issued a ticket. You must pay the fine at any Costa Rican bank before you depart the country. If you choose not to pay you may have problems leaving. Costa Rica is more advanced than the other Central American countries and the chance of them catching you is relatively high.

Costa Rica/Leaving Car

Costa Rica is the only country on the trip that does not stamp your vehicle into your passport. If you decide to leave your car in Costa Rica, hop on a plane and travel home in luxury. However, when you return to the country in the future your abandoned jalopy may present problems.

Shipping Your From or To Costa Rica

You have driven over 4000 miles and you don't want to drive back. No problem, ship your car home! There are two main ports in Costa Rica. If you are shipping your car to the Pacific side of the US or Canada you must ship it out of Puerto Caldera. For shipments to the Atlantic coast the port is Puerto Limon. First you must find the Aduana office which is located in the main shipping building at each port. Go to the Aduana and tell them that you would like to ship you vehicle to the United States. The paperwork and the assistance of the Aduana official will cost between $300 and $400.

The official will file all the necessary paperwork and arrange to have your vehicle placed in a shipping container. The official will also do the leg work and contact the shipping agency for booking the container on to a ship. The actual cost of shipping is between $1500.00 and $2000.00. Once the paperwork is done you must go back to San Jose and sign the release forms at the shipping company's office. You may pay for the shipment at the opposite end, when you return, but the Aduana fees must be paid in Costa Rica.

You also have the option of a non-container shipment. This means that your car is placed on to the deck of some ship and strapped down. The cost is cheaper, but the chances of damage and theft are much greater.

The procedures for shipping a car to Costa Rica are basically the same. However, when you ship a vehicle to Costa Rica you must get your car out of Customs, which is a total nightmare. Pick up a copy of the Tico Times for information about clearing Customs and hiring brokers to assist you with the legalities.

Consider the cost and formalities of shipping your vehicle. After paying shipping fees and purchasing your return ticket you will have paid close to double the cost of driving back—the decision is yours!

Costa Rica/Long Term Travel

You may drive in Costa Rica for six months without any type of "in-country" registration, however you most update your visa and car insurance accordingly. For most this means departing the country after 90 days for 72 hours and then returning. It is much easier to leave the country by bus to Nicaragua or Panama for a few days and then to return for your new entry stamp. Otherwise you will have to check your vehicle and person in and out of each country—remember, your entry by vehicle is not indicated in your passport and therefore you may go by other transportation to Nicaragua or Panama to extend your visa. If you didn't get a chance to see San Juan del Sur in Nicaragua take care of your extension at the border and spend a few days in San Juan.

Costa Rica Living

By now, most people throughout the world are familiar with Costa Rica as a tourist destination. Ecologically sensitive, democratically stable, peaceful, Costa Rica enjoys the reputation as an almost ideal location to spend a few days, weeks, or months basking in a tropical paradise. Recently, Costa Rica has been "discovered" internationally as an attractive retirement destination as well.

Costa Rica is the only Central American country to enjoy complete democratization since 1948. Being incredibly far-sighted, the leadership at that time demilitarized the country, rejecting a standing army in favor of providing for its people the fundamentals of equality, justice, liberty and freedom. Even before the installation of a democratic constitution and the rejection of a standing military, Costa Rica's leaders historically provided for the health and welfare of the people. Universal health care, agricultural reforms and housing programs were all in effect before the turn of the century, reflecting the country's true heart and serving as a blueprint for other Latin American countries to follow.

As an affordable retirement destination, Costa Rica offers a variety of means to acquire legal residency. As a legal resident, the retiree enjoys the freedoms and most of the important rights of native Costa Ricans—health care, insurance, et cetera. While the Costa Rican government has recently passed several new tax laws, few will impact on the retiree. On a sour note, many of the "perks" which were associated with foreign retirees living in Costa Rica were repealed three years ago. These included duty-free importation of household goods and a duty-free car every five years. However, to off-set this, the duties on most of these items have decreased and will continue to decrease for the next several years.

Regulations concerning retirees and residency are covered under Costa Rican Law Number 4812, passed in July, 1971. The "Resident Annuitants and Resident Pensioners Law" allows for people with guaranteed incomes to become legal residents. The law's two parts, the "Rentista" and the "Pensionado," differ only in the amount of money required.

For the "Rentista" (someone living in Costa Rica but not "retired"), the dollar amount which must be available for conversion to colones each month is US$1,000.00 guaranteed, in a stable and permanent way, by a first rate bank and for a minimum period of five years. Any person over the age of 18 may apply for the status of "Rentista." The "Pensionado" (someone actually retired), must have a guaranteed US$600.00 monthly generated through a verifiable pension fund such as Social Security, private company retirement plan, IRA, or other retirement fund, and available to the retiree for life.

Application for residency under this law requires a number of ancillary documents--ancillary, that is, to primary documentation of funds available from the appropriate source. These are:

• Birth certificate of the applicant, spouse, and any children who may be migrating as part of the family.
• Marriage certificate, if applicable.
• Certification from a law enforcement agency (with associated finger print cards) verifying no police record.
• Certified photocopies of all pages of the applicant's passport (and the passports of all family members involved in the migration).
• Twelve passport-size photos (six front and six profile) of each person involved.
• All documents should be originals, except where noted, and must be authenticated with the appropriate documentation stamps, by the closest Costa Rican Consul or Embassy. Cost for this authentication varies but will run around US$40 to US$50 per page as of this writing.
Residency applications under this law are processed by the Costa Rican Tourist Board and usually take no more than six months. Neither Rentistas nor Pensiona-

dos can work as paid employees. However, work is permitted if the resident is a share-holder in a Costa Rican company and/or is a company's legal representative. Also, a Rentista or Pensionado should plan on living in Costa Rica a minimum of four months a year although this provision may be waived under special circumstances.

Other than residency, there are many questions a person may have about retiring here—concerning transportation to and within the country, health care, banking and postal services, taxes—let's consider a few of the most common. Transportation within the country is hampered only by poor roads and wildly enthusiastic drivers. Rental cars are plentiful and new and used cars are available for purchase—at a premium. Buses and taxis run throughout the country and are an affordable, and scenic, way to travel on a budget.

For the retiree, health care is critical. Costa Rica has one of the finest health care systems in the world and it is available to all at affordable costs. Health insurance can be purchased through the national insurance company and premiums are roughly one fifth those of equal coverage in the States. Residents may join the national social security system (Caja Costarricense de Seguro Social—CCSS) for a minimal monthly cost and enjoy the universal health care Costa Rican citizens enjoy. Most doctors in Costa Rica have received training in the United States or Europe and are highly qualified. Firsts for many major operations in Latin America have been performed here. Costa Rica has both private and public health care systems. Both are manned by the same doctors and the overall quality is almost equal—a patient in a private clinic or hospital will receive more attention than one in a public hospital.

Costa Rica's mail service does not have a good reputation. Theft of valuables is rampant, undeliverable mail is common, and service to the public is spotty, at best. Efforts are being made to improve the system, but so far little improvement is evident. Many private mail services exist and are serviceable. Connecting Costa Rica with the US Postal Service, these private carriers provide a relatively safe alternative to the Costa Rican Correo.

Death and Taxes are inevitable. However, retirees in Costa Rica are spared from the "taxes" part. Neither Rentistas nor Pensionados are taxed except for municipal services and real property, both at a very affordable level. Sales taxes have risen during the past year to the current 15% on most consumer goods. There is a canasta básica (basic basket) which contains more than 700 items exempt from sales tax, tremendously benefiting those on fixed incomes. Overall, the tax burden for those living in Costa Rica is small.

Housing options are many in Costa Rica from mansions of several thousand square feet to small, unassuming cottages. Prices are generally lower than those in the States or Europe, though in many highly desirable areas housing costs are way above the norms. Several retirement projects are in the works for Costa Rica and will fill a niche in the affordable housing market here. There are reliable real estate brokers who can help find the perfect retirement home.

If you're not yet ready to retire, you may be able to take advantage of Costa Rican Law Number 7033 passed in August, 1986. The "General Law of Immigration and Foreigners" provides guidelines for residency as an "investor" in the Costa Rican economy. Under this law an applicant must be able to demonstrate, through a feasibility study or other verifiable documentation, that an investment of US$200,000 (minimum) has been made or will be made in one of these areas:

. ornamental plants or flowers
. leather products or derivatives
. spices and/or condiments
. fruits
. fresh vegetables
. processed foods
. wood or wood derivatives
. agroindustrial projects that will utilize agriculture, cattle, fishing or forestry raw products and that require a procedure of industrial transformation industrial mining projects
. projects for the production of capital goods, consumption and consumer products for the support of exportation and investment in Costa Rica
. If a project directly involves tourism or reforestation (or other special projects considered to be in the national interest under special regulations) the investment requirement is only US$50,000.

Documentation for application under this law is practically the same as for the law governing "rentistas" and "pensionados" except for the additional required documentation of the investment. Approval for application under the General Law of Immigration and Foreigners is through two separate agencies: the Center for Promotion of Exterior Commerce (PROCOMER) and the general immigration office. Final approval can take several months and is more uncertain and complicated than the law covering retirees.

Should a foreigner marry a Costa Rican citizen, the right to apply for residency accompanies the ceremony. Residency is not automatic; the non-Costa Rican spouse must apply to the Immigration and Naturalization office to become a resident. In this case, the necessary documents are: birth certificate (or certified copy), copy of passport, and an official copy of the marriage certificate. The wait for approval varies, but is usually quite short.

With somewhat more ambiguity, the case of documented blood ties, or consanguinity, to a Costa Rican citizen may entitle a foreigner to be considered for residency. The documentation required in this case is often complex and/or confusing and consultation with a qualified attorney is most important.

If a person is interested in obtaining his or her Costa Rican residency, regardless of under which law, the advice and assistance of an efficient and qualified attorney is strongly suggested. A list of such attorneys can be solicited from the American Embassy in Costa Rica.

Costa Rica/Selling Car

Good luck selling your car in Costa Rica! The laws on selling used vehicles seem to change daily in Costa Rica. Most likely you won't make any money when you sell your vehicle.

If you do so, you need to place your vehicle into a Customs Storage Warehouse, find your buyer, and let your buyer handle the Customs duty and purchase Costa Rican license plates. The government adds a 30-50% sales tax that substantially decreases your profit and there are additional fees for registering vehicles. There are stories that registering a vehicle is more expensive than the actual value of the vehicle's original purchase price. All that said, here is our updated information for selling a car in 2011.

While it is possible for you to sell your car after driving to Costa Rica, possibly even make some profit, it is certainly not without its difficulties. The average customs tax on cars in C.R. is close to 55% of what an American would consider to be the value. For example, if the car you drive here is worth $10,000 in the U.S.A., expect the customs tax to be at least $5,500.00. Also, Costa Rica has their own government "blue book" that is not at all similar to the Kelley's in the U.S.A. If you have leather seats, air conditioning, automatic transmission, anything that Costa Rica considers a luxury the cost is even more. Additionally, the inspection process has become tedious: tires cannot be wider by even an inch then the side of the car, a chip in the windshield has to be fixed, and the exhaust is carefully analyzed. This being said, it is entirely possible to sell the car without ever paying any of these taxes or going through this inspection process at all.

We have in place a network which can advertise and sell your car, given it is of a style that is even somewhat acceptable here (please contact us for advice). Some things you'll need to know before selling your vehicle:

> sending us photos or the vehicle
> your approximate selling price
> the year
> the motor size
> transmission type
> the date you expect to have the car in Costa Rica
> and the mileage on the vehicle
> copy of the title
> It is also possible for you to leave the car in one of our representative's possession when you return to the states for us to sell for you should you not wish to wait for the sale to take place.

Driving your vehicle to Costa Rica does have distinct advantages over shipping it. Any car that that is brought in by a tourist by driving, is given a 90 day grace period (similar to that of your personal passport) to leave the country or become registered in Costa Rica. Should you choose to ship your vehicle, something we can help with as well, you can expect to pay customs tax immediately upon arrival or risk the government putting the vehicle into storage and charging a daily charge against the value of the vehicle. Once the daily charge exceeds the value of the vehicle, the government auctions the car at a ridiculously low price and you are just out. The cost for driving your vehicle across the border into Costa Rica is very inexpensive. You are required to purchase liability insurance from the government, at a cost of about $35 dollars for your 90 day stay. There is the traditional, "oh no, it has a bug on the grill" spraying charge of a few dollars, but the rest of the procedure is relatively painless. Should you wish to keep your vehicle in Costa Rica after the 90 days, we strongly advise that you hire a company like ours to assist you in the import duty process as a personal representation with customs can save you a lot of money.

Bringing Vehicles to Costa Rica

If you are traveling to Costa Rica with your vehicle (cars, trucks, and/or motorcycles), either used or new, you must carry the original title of your vehicle at all times.

If you want to stay in Costa Rica for a few weeks to travel around or drive through, you will be issued a three month temporary vehicle use permit and you will not be required to pay your vehicle's Customs duty.

Once your three month temporary vehicle use permit expires, you can only renew it one more time for three additional months at any Customs Office and pay no vehicle's Customs duties.

Once your renew use permit expires, you either must leave the country or must store your vehicle in a Customs storage warehouse where your vehicle will remain until you pay the Customs duties and purchase Costa Rican license plates. If you are considering staying in Costa Rica with your vehicle for more than six months, importing your vehicle to Costa Rica, or selling your vehicle while in Costa Rica, please read the following:

Required Documents

In order to bring your motor vehicle (cars, trucks, and/or motorcycles) either used or new to Costa Rica, you will be required to provide the following documents:

a. Original title of your car
b. Bill of lading (if it is shipped)

c. Vehicle Emission Control Certificate (*) issued by an Emission Inspection Station (Garage Repair Shop, Gas Station, etc.) certified by the Department of Motor Vehicles (DMV) of your State or by the vehicle manufacturer (only if vehicle is new), translated into Spanish by an Official Translator, and authenticated by the Consulate of Costa Rica nearest to the Emission Inspection Station that issued your certificate

(*) Vehicle Emission Control Certificates are issued after thorough emission testing and inspection to vehicles in compliance with the U.S. federal standards for carbon monoxide pollution.

Certificates may acquire different names depending on the State that you live in. For example, in the State of California Vehicle Emission Control Certificates are also called Smog Certificates.

Customs Duty

Vehicles imported into Costa Rica, whether new or used, either for personal use or for sale, are generally dutiable at the following rates based on your vehicle's customs appraised value, and its age (the number of years that the vehicle has from its date of manufacture to the date that goes through Customs.)

> Vehicles from 0 to 3 years old 59.33%
> Vehicles from 4 to 5 years old 70.63%
> Vehicles more than 6 years old 85.32%

Calculating Customs Duty

The dutiable amount of your vehicle is calculated as follows

> Customs Duty = (VCAV) * CDP%
> VCAV: Vehicle's Customs Appraised Value
> CDP%: Customs Duty Percentage

Vehicle's Customs Appraised Value

Your Vehicle's Customs Appraised Value (VCAV) is calculated by adding your vehicle's market value, your vehicle's freight, and your vehicle's freight insurance.
VCAV = VMV + F + FI

VMV: Vehicle's Market Value

F: Freight

FI: Freight Insurance

Vehicle's Market Value (VMV):

Customs use the Black Book Guide, a US Consumer Research Magazine that establishes the current market value of vehicles worldwide, to appraise your vehicle based on the model and its manufacture date. The Black Book Guide provides two market prices for vehicles: The wholesale price and the retail price. Customs will use the wholesale price if you are a car/motorcycle dealer and/or import company. Otherwise, they will use the retail price of your vehicle.

You may show your invoice if you purchase your vehicle recently. However, Customs may reject prices shown on an invoice at their own discretion.

Freight (F):

It is the cost of transporting your vehicle from your country to Costa Rica. Customs will look at your bill of lading in order to determine that. If there is no bill of lading and/or you drove your vehicle from a country to Costa Rica, your freight will be equaled to 7% (seven percent) of the market value of your vehicle according to the Black Book Guide. Customs will abide by this formula:

$$\text{Freight} = \text{VMV} * 0.07$$

VMV: Vehicle's Market Value

Freight Insurance (FI):

It is the amount of money that you pay to insure your vehicle.

If you did not pay any insurance, Customs will calculate the insurance as follows:

Customs will take your vehicle's market value according to the Black Book Guide, then add the amount of money of the freight. Multiply by 110% and then by 1.5% (see formula):

Freight Insurance = (VMV + F) * 1.10 * 0.015
VMV: Vehicle's Market Value   F: Freight

Custom Duty Percentage (CDP%) Once Customs appraise your vehicle, they will use that amount to calculate the percentage that your vehicle must pay in order to enter Costa Rica.

The Customs duty percentage is determined by the age of your vehicle that is calculated by adding the number of years between the date of manufacture of your vehicle and the date that your vehicle goes through Customs in Costa Rica.

If your vehicle is from 0 to 3 years old, the duty rate is 59.33% of the total value of your vehicle for Customs Duty Purposes.

If your vehicle is from 4 to 5 years old, the duty rate is 70.63% of the total value of your vehicle for Customs Duty Purposes.

If your vehicle is more than 6 years old, the duty rate is 85.32% of the total value of your vehicle for Customs Duty Purposes.

TIME	CUSTOMS FORMULA	DUTY RATE
0-3	(VCAV * 0.5933)	85.32%
4-5	(VCAV * 0.7063)	70.63%
6+	(VCAV * 0.8532)	59.33%

Time

Number of years between the date that your car was manufactured and the time that your car is passing through customs in Costa Rica.

Customs Formula

Formula that Customs will use to calculate the duties that you must pay for your vehicle.

Duty Rate

Percentage that Customs charge for letting your car into Costa Rica.

Example I: You pay for shipping and insurance For example, if you have a BMW 750iL Sedan 4D manufactured in 1998 and you are a person—not a company- bringing a car into Costa Rica, you shipped your car from Miami, Florida to Puerto Limon, Limon, Costa Rica, and you are bringing the car into Costa Rica in 1999. Your freight from Miami, Florida, U.S.A. to Puerto Limon, Limon, Costa Rica cost $700.00, and the Freight insurance cost $150.00

Customs will calculate the customs duties using its formula as follows:

Customs Duty = VCAV * CDP

Since VCAV = (VMV + F + FI) **VMV:** Vehicle's Market Value According to Black Book Guide's suggested retail price as of August 1999: $69,700.00

F: The freight from Miami, Florida to Puerto Limon, Limon, Costa Rica was $700.00

FI: The Freight insurance was $150.00

Then, your Vehicle's Appraised Value is: $70,550

CDP (Custom Duty Percentage):

Since your car is 1 year old, customs will apply the following formula:

Formula: Customs Duty = VCAV * 0.5933

Customs Duty = $70,550.00 * 0.5933 Customs Duty = $41,857.31

You will have to pay an amount equaled to $41,857.31 US dollars to bring your car into Costa Rica

Costa Rica/Real Estate
www.ticotimes.net

Check the above link for a current listing of Real Estate for sale in Costa Rica. Additionally, there are several Real Estate companies representing sellers/buyers in the tourist areas with websites listings, such as Century 21 and Remax.

It is advisable that if you are truly interested in investing in real estate in CR you should visit the area and spend a good amount of time getting to know the pace of life in the particular region that you have chosen.

Most Real Estate prices listed by real estate companies in CR are extravagantly high. To get a DEAL one must travel outside the tourist areas and negotiate with the locals.

Currency: Costa Rican colón

Meals
BUDGET: US$2-5
MID-RANGE: US$5-10
TOP-END: US$10 and upwards

Lodging
BUDGET: US$3-10
MIDRANGE: US$10-20
TOP-END: US$20 and upwards

Costa Rica isn't as cheap as some of its neighbors, but it's definitely a budget destination. If you're traveling with someone, you should be able to scrape by on US$12 a day, but US$20 is probably more realistic. If you're planning to have your own bathroom, eat decently and catch an occasional plane, US$25-50 should cover your needs. Travelers expecting to be very comfortable can easily spend US$50-150 per day, depending on their definition of comfort. The best tours cost upwards of US$200 per day, but these include flights and first-class accommodations and services.

If you want to change cash, stick to US dollars (but make sure they're in decent condition and avoid US$100 bills—due to a counterfeiting scam, most Costa Ricans won't touch them). US dollars are your best bet for traveler's checks as well, as other currencies will rarely be accepted—any of the major brands will do. If you buy colones with your credit card, expect to get hit with a huge interest bill. It's increasingly easy to find ATMs, even in small towns, though some banks, like branches of Banco Nacional, accept cards held by their customers only.

You don't usually need to bother with tipping at restaurants, as most add a 10% tip (plus 15% tax) to the bill. You should tip bellboys and room cleaners about US$0.50, tour guides US$1-5 a day per person. Of course, if the service is excellent or lousy you should use your own discretion.

Top Five Google Search For 'Costa Rica'

http://www.visitcostarica.com/
http://www.tourism-costarica.com/
http://travel.state.gov/travel/cis_pa_tw/cis/cis_1093.html
http://en.wikipedia.org/wiki/Costa_Rica
http://www.lonelyplanet.com/costa-ricagoogle.com

Top Three Google Search 'Drive To Costa Rica'

http://www.frommers.com/destinations/costarica/0219020009.html
http://www.costaricamap.com/ing/infomanejar.html
http://www.ticotravel.com/faqdrive.htm

Chapter
seven
Panama

Building things partially is a strange concept in Latin America, building things half way is common. Usually this is OK but when you come cross a bridge you want it NOT to be one of those projects.

"Love is friendship, set on fire."
- Jeremy Taylor

P anama's arts reflect its ethnic mix. Indian tribes, West Indian groups, mestizos, Chinese, Middle Eastern, Swiss, Yugoslav and North American immigrants have all contributed ingredients to the cultural stew. Traditional arts include wood carving, weaving, ceramics and mask-making.

Spanish is the official language, though US influence and the international nature of the canal zone reinforce the use of English as a second language. West Indian immigrants also speak Caribbean-accented English. Indian tribes have retained their own languages. Panama is predominantly Roman Catholic, but there are sizable Muslim and Protestant minorities and small numbers of Hindus and Jews.

Environment

The Isthmus of Panama is the umbilical cord joining South and Central America. It borders Costa Rica to the west and Colombia to the east. Panama's arched shape reflects both its role as a bridge between continents and as a passageway between oceans. At its narrowest point, it is only 50km (30mi) wide, but it has a 1160km (720mi) Caribbean coastline on its northern shore and a 1690km (1048mi) Pacific coast to the south. The famous canal is 80km (50mi) long and effectively divides the country into eastern and western regions.

There are hundreds of islands near the Panamanian coasts. The two major archipelagos are the San Blas and Bocas del Toro chains in the Caribbean Sea, though the best snorkeling, diving and deep-sea fishing are to be found in the Pacific near Coiba Island and the Pearl Islands. Panama has flat coastal lowlands and two mountain chains running along its spine. The highest peak is Volcán Barú at 3475m (11,400ft).

Rainforests dominate the canal zone, the northwestern portion of the country and much of the eastern half. Although Costa Rica is widely known for its fantastic wildlife, Panama has, in fact, a greater number of flora and fauna species, more land set aside for preservation and far fewer people wandering through the jungle looking for wildlife and inadvertently scaring it away. There's much truth in the Panamanian saying that in Costa Rica 20 tourists try to see one resplendent quetzal, but in Panama one person tries to see 20 of these exquisite birds.

Panama has two seasons. The dry season lasts from January to mid-April and the rainy season from mid-April to December. Rainfall is heavier on the Caribbean side of the highlands, though most people live on or near the Pacific coast. Temperatures are typically hot in the lowlands (between 21°C and 32°C/70°F and 90°F) and cool in the mountains (between 10-18°C/50-64°F). These vary little throughout the year.

General Information

Panama offers some of the finest snorkeling, birding and deep-sea fishing in the world, so it's hard to figure out why travelers tend to steer clear of this country or just whiz through on their way to or from South America. It may have something to do with the fact that Panama is known internationally for its canal, the 1989 US invasion and the name it donated to a style of headgear, but this does it no justice.

The reality is a proud prosperous nation that honors its seven Indian tribes and its rich Spanish legacy and embraces visitors so enthusiastically that it's difficult to leave without feeling that you're in on a secret that the rest of the traveling world will one day uncover.

Warning

Panama City is safer than most capital cities, but some parts of it (particularly the district of Chorrillo) should not be strolled around at night. The city of Colón has a major crime problem and absolutely shouldn't be strolled around day or night. The area of Darién Province between Yaviza and the Colombian border along the upper Tuira River is particularly unsafe due to the presence of smugglers, bandits and Colombian guerrillas and paramilitary forces. However, the vast majority of Darién National Park is relatively safe, though it's advisable to visit the park with a guide due to the inherent risks of travel in remote jungle with ill-defined trails. As the situation in Colombia continues to destabilize, it's advisable to keep your ear as close to the ground as possible while planning any off-the-beaten-path expeditions.

FULL COUNTRY NAME: Republic of Panama
AREA: 78,000 sq km (30,420 sq mi)
POPULATION: 2.8 milion (growth rate 1.3%)
CAPITAL CITY: Panama City (pop 700,000)
PEOPLE: 65% mestizo, 14% African descent, 10% Spanish descent, 10% Indian
LANGUAGE: Spanish, English and Indian languages
RELIGION: 85% Roman Catholic, 10% Protestant, 5% Islamic
GOVERNMENT: Constitutional republic
PRESIDENT: Mireya Moscoso
GDP: US$21 billion
GDP PER HEAD: US$7,600
ANNUAL GROWTH: 4.4%
INFLATION: 1.5%
MAJOR INDUSTRIES: Banking, construction, petroleum refining, brewing, cement and other construction materials, sugar milling, shipping and agriculture
MAJOR TRADING PARTNERS: USA, EU, Central America & Caribbean, Japan
Panama Currency: US dollar (known as 'balboa')

Meals
BUDGET: US$2-5
MID-RANGE: US$5-10
TOP-END: US$10+

Lodging
BUDGET: US$7-16
MIDRANGE: US$16-20
TOP-END: US$20+

Accommodation tends to be more expensive in Panama than in other parts of Central America; a hotel room that might cost US$6 in Nicaragua or Guatemala might cost US$10 here. If you're traveling on a budget, you'll pay at least US$15 per day for a room and three meals. A moderate budget will be in the range of US$20-30 a day.

Panama uses the US dollar as its currency. The official name for it is the balboa, but it's exactly the same bill. Panamanian coins are of the same value, size and metal as US coins; both are used. In most of Central America, US dollars are the only currency exchanged. In Panama City, however, you can exchange currencies from almost anywhere in the world at a casa de cambio, due to the city's large international offshore banking industry.

You can tip some small change, or around 10% of the bill if you're feeling affluent, in fancier restaurants; in small cafes and more casual places, tipping is not necessary. Haggling over prices is not the general custom in Panama.

Panama City

The capital of Panama is a modern, thriving commercial center stretching 10km (6mi) along the Pacific coast from the ruins of Panamá Viejo in the east to the edge of the Panama Canal in the west. The old district of San Felipe (also known as Casco Antiguo or Casco Viejo) juts into the sea on the southwestern side of town. It's an area of decaying colonial grandeur, striking architecture, peeling paint and decrepit balconies. Attractions include the 17th-century Metropolitan Church, the Interoceanic Canal Museum of Panama, the Plaza de Bolívar, the presidential palace, the History Museum of Panama and the sea wall built by the Spaniards four centuries ago. Via España's banking district is the complete opposite to this yesteryear charm, with aggressively modern buildings and sophisticated entertainments.

Attractions on the fringes of the city include the Panama Canal, the 16th-century ruins of Panamá Viejo, the Summit Botanical Gardens and Zoo, the tropical rain forest of the Parque Nacional Sobreranía and the 265-hectare (655-acre) Parque Nacional Metropolitana.

Panama Canal

The Canal is both an engineering marvel and one of the most significant waterways on earth. Stretching 80km (50mi) from Panama City on the Pacific coast to Colón on the Atlantic side, it provides passage for over 12,000 oceangoing vessels per year. Seeing a huge ship nudge its way through the narrow canal, with vast tracts of virgin jungle on both sides, is an unforgettable sight. The easiest and best way to visit the Canal is to go to the Miraflores Locks, on the northeastern fringe of Panama City, where a platform offers visitors a good view of the locks in operation. There's also a museum with a model and a film about the Canal. Boats leave Balboa, a western suburb of Panama City, for a five-hour tour through the locks to Miraflores Lake.

Isla Taboga

This charming and historical island, 20km (12mi) south of Panama City, has an attractive beach, some lovely protected rain forest, and is home to one of the largest colonies of brown pelicans in Latin America. Known as the Island of Flowers, because at certain times of the year it is filled with the aroma of sweet-smelling blooms, the island is a favorite retreat from the city. Taboga has a long history and was settled even before Panama City. There is a small church here, claimed to be second oldest in the Western Hemisphere, and Pizarro set sail from here for Peru in 1524. The island's annual festival is July 16, and involves nautical processions and celebrations. Taboga is a one-hour boat trip from Balboa.

Boquete

Known for its cool, fresh climate and pristine natural environment, the small alpine town of Boquete is nestled into a craggy mountain valley 35km (22mi) north of David. It's a fine place for walking, bird watching, horse riding and enjoying a respite from the heat of the lowlands. Flowers, coffee and citrus fruits are grown in the area and the town's Feria de las Flores y del Cafe is a popular annual festival held in January. Boquete is a good base for climbing 3475m (11,400ft) Volcán Barú, 15km (9mi) west, or visiting the volcano's 14,300-hectare (35,320-acre) national park

Top Five Google Search For 'Panama'

http://en.wikipedia.org/wiki/Panama

http://www.state.gov/r/pa/ei/bgn/2030.htm

http://www.panamainfo.com/

http://news.bbc.co.uk/2/hi/americas/country_profiles/1229332.stm

http://www.pancanal.com/eng/photo/camera-java.html

Top Three Google Search 'Drive To Panama'

http://www.yourpanama.com/drive-to-panama.html

http://www.panamainfo.com/en/faq-the-most-frequently-asked-questions-about-travel-panama

http://boards.independenttraveler.com/showthread.php?12043-tips-or-advise-griving-to-Panama

Chapter eight
Health Tips

Don't drink the water—seems to be the best advice no matter where you are in Central America.

"Women don't want to hear what you think. Women want to hear what they think - in a deeper voice."
- Bill Cosby

Comment

For short term visitors, catching one of the various diseases that often attack the poor within the slums is a rarity. Of course, you do need to exercise precaution concerning what you eat as well as general personal cleanliness. Condoms should be used in all sexual contacts, AIDS cases have substantially increased over the last several years among the prostitute population. Malaria and dengue, caused by insect bites, continue to be the most common diseases throughout Central America. There are no vaccination requirements for Mexico and Central America and none are recommended for short term visitors.

Vaccinations

For those staying longer than two months you might consider a visit to your doctor. Check out the new Hepatitis A vaccine, it requires only two inoculations rather than the older one that requires several boosters regularly. Consider this vaccination seriously if you plan to spend a great amount of time in the bush.

The anti-malaria drug chloroquine should also be considered and it is available from most pharmacies in Central America. Chloroquine makes some people ill and the various brands have different affects on different people. Thus if one brand makes you ill, try another.

A tetanus shot should also be considered. Most childhood vaccinations are good for five years. If your overdo, get one before you leave.

Leishmanioses

This disease has afflicted primarily the North Coast of Honduras and it is carried by the female sand fly. Health officials recommend that visitors wear insect repellent and protective clothing if they plan to be outdoors for long periods of time. Leishmanioses is treatable.

Malaria

Malaria is carried by the female mosquito and afflicts those areas in lower altitudes. It is characterized by high fevers, chills, headaches, and fatigue. It can be prevented by taking an anti-malarial drug such as chloroquine. People traveling to lower altitudes should apply generous amounts of insect repellent, wear protective clothing, and use mosquito netting while sleeping. Chloroquine should be started two weeks before travel and must be continued for several weeks after travel. Malaria is treatable.

Dengue

Dengue is an acute tropical disease transmitted by mosquitoes. It is characterized by high fever, rash, headache and severe muscle and joint pain. Dengue is treatable, but painful. It is common throughout the native population in Central America.

If you should be unfortunate enough to contract malaria or dengue or any of the above diseases, don't panic, they can be treated and usually are all over in about a week.

Medical care varies in quality. Doctors and hospitals often expect immediate cash payment for services. US medical insurance usually covers emergency medical treatments. However, the Health Insurance Association of America says you may be out of luck if your injury or illness is not an emergency. This Washington-based outfit suggests you check with your health provider, or consider buying insurance for your next trip. Companies like Access America and Worldwide Assistance Services sell travel insurance. On the plus side, however, medical visits are very inexpensive as compared to the US. Prescription drugs are often available over the counter or payment of a small fee to a physician.

Drug stores are readily available and take turns being open at night. Ask a resident to find out which one is open (turno). Major pharmacies are able to fill just about any prescription. Many pharmacists speak English.

The **Center for Disease Control** in Atlanta has a FAX information service from which you can get specific information. To get information call 404-332-4565 and follow the prompts (touch tone). They have multiple information about regions and specific diseases. The bulletin for health risks in Central America is #220160 and it's 8 pages. They also have a specific bulletin for dengue fever #221030 (one page). The number for their table of contents bulletin is #000005. Have your fax number ready when you call and be sure the machine is ready.

The Center for Disease Control international hot line is (404) 332-4559 and (404) 639-1610 or here on the net http://www.cdc.gov

Tap water

Tap water is not safe to drink. If you have a portable means of purifying, it can be helpful in rural areas where bottled water may not be available. Often when Central Americans refer to potable water, what they really mean is indoor plumbing rather than the quality or drinkability (sic) of the water. Water treatment is planned for the future in many areas, but it is years away. Our suggestion to short term visitors is don't drink water, even in the luxury resorts, try and stick to hot coffee and bottled drinks (beer, colas, juices, whatever). And even with all the precautions you might take, you might still wind up with Montezumas' or Lempiras' Revenge. One hundred percent safety is never possible.

Worried About Travel Abroad?

You can easily consult with the U. S. State Department about current travel conditions. The State Department's Bureau of Consular Affairs maintains a recorded message detailing current travel advisories for different regions of the world. You'll need a touch-tone phone to navigate through the instructions to hear about the country of interest. The phone number is (202) 647-5225. These advisories are also available from on-line systems as well as the Internet.

Final Words

Have a fantastic trip! If you have additional information that you would like to share with me for future editions of this publication please send them to info@ drivemeloco.com

Mexcian Proverbs

"It is not the fault of the mouse but of the one who offers him the cheese"
~ Mexican Proverb

"A person born to be a flower pot will not go beyond the porch"
~ Mexican Proverb

"Tell me who your friends are and I'll tell you who you are."
~ Mexican Proverb

"A good resolution is like an old horse, which is often saddled but rarely ridden"
Mexican Proverb

"I never ask God to give me anything; I only ask him to put me where things are"
~ Mexican Proverb

Chapter
nine
SPANISH SURVIVAL

This picture was taken in Cuba, though it isn't part of 'this' trip I feel the message is universal and is a wonderful reminder for how to live and travel.

"Money won't create success. The freedom to make it will."
- Nelson Mandela

Comment

Spanish is a beautiful language, take some time before your travels and, at the very least, go over the basics of the language. A basic knowledge of the idiom will lead to a more fulfilling experience. However, for those travelers that have no knowledge of Spanish or for those travelers that need a quick refresher course the following tables provide survival type skills.

In Latin American countries there is a big difference between the "tu" form and the "usted" form. The former used with friends and people of acquaintance and the latter used when speaking with officials, elders or other people of respect. The following tables display both forms where appropriate, the white face ☺ symbolizes the "tu" form and the black face ☺ symbolizes the form to use in respectful conversations, the "usted" form.

USEFUL EXPRESSIONS — EXPRESIONES ÚTILES

USEFUL EXPRESSIONS	EXPRESIONES ÚTILES
I don't speak much Spanish	No hablo mucho español
Do you speak English?	¿☺Habla usted, ☺hablas español?
Slower, please	Más despacio, por favor
Could you repeat?	¿☺Puede repetir?, ☺Puedes repetir?
Thank you	Gracias
Thank you very much	Muchas gracias
You're welcome	De nada
Sorry	Perdón, ☺Perdone, ☺Perdona
Excuse me	Permiso, ☺Disculpe, ☺Disculpa
Okay, all right	Vale, de acuerdo
Very well	Muy bien
Perfect	Perfecto
I agree, I don't agree	Estoy de acuerdo, no estoy de acuerdo
To your health	Salud

Enjoy your meal	Buen provecho, Que aproveche
Could you help me?	¿☺Me puede , ☺me puedes ayudar?
May I take a picture?	¿Puedo sacar una fotografía?
I don't know	No sé, no lo sé
I don't understand	No entiendo
I don't like it	No me gusta
What time is it?	¿Qué hora es?
Help	Ayuda, Socorro
Come in	Adelante, ☺Pase, ☺Pasa
Pardon me	☺Disculpe, ☺Dispense, ☺Disculpa
Of course	Por supuesto

MEETING PEOPLE

SALUDOS Y DESPEDIDAS

Hello	Hola
How are you?, How do you do?	¿☺Cómo está usted? ¿ ☺Cómo estás?
How are things going?	¿Qué tal?, ¿Qué tal todo?
Fine, thank you	Bien, gracias
Very well, very badly	Muy bien, muy mal
Good morning	Buenos días
Good afternoon, evening	Buenas tardes
Good night	Buenas noches
See you	Nos vemos
See you soon, later	Hasta pronto, hasta luego
Good bye	Adios
Nice to meet you	Encantado de ☺conocerle, ☺conocerte
What is your name?	¿☺Cómo se llama usted?, ¿☺Cómo te llamas?
My name is ...	Mi nombre es..., me llamo...
I am American, from America	Soy americano, soy de América
I would like to introduce you to	☺Le presento a..., ☺te presento a...
A pleasure	Mucho gusto, un placer

WHAT DO I EAT TODAY ? COMIDA Y BEBIDA

I 'm hungry	Tengo hambre
I 'm thirsty	Tengo sed
I feel like an ice cream, chips	Me apetece un helado, patatas fritas...
I like vegetables, eggs...	Me gustan las verduras, los huevos...
I don't like soup, pasta...	No me gusta la sopa, la pasta...
I love fruits, fish...	Me encanta la fruta, el pescado...
I hate meat, milk, rice...	Odio la carne, la leche, el arroz...
I would like to try the dessert	Quisiera probar el postre
Will you bring me some water?	¿☺Podría, ☺podrías traerme agua?
I will have some wine, a spirit?	Tomaré vino, un refresco...
Could you bring me the menu?	¿☺Puede, ☺puedes traer el menú?
What is for breakfast, lunch, dinner?	¿Qué hay de desayunar, comer, cenar?
Where is the closest restaurant?	¿Dónde está el restaurante más cercano?
What is the typical meal in this area?	¿Cuál es la comida típica de esta zona?
I would like to make a reservation	Quisiera hacer una reserva
Fork, spoon, knife	Cuchara, tenedor, cuchillo

WHERE AM I?   TUARSE

How long does it take to go to...?	¿Cuánto se tarda en ir a...?
Am I close to the city center?	¿Estoy cerca del centro de la ciudad?
Which is the shortest path to go to..?	¿Cuál es el camino más corto para ir a...?
Could you tell me where is...?	¿☺Me puede, ☺me puedes decir dónde está...?
I'm looking for the tourist office	Estoy buscando la oficina de información
Do I go straight ahead...?	¿Sigo recto?
Do I turn to the left, right?	¿Giro a la izquierda, a la derecha?
The airport, train station, bus station	El aeropuerto, la estación de trenes, de autobuses
A hotel, a pension, the market	Un hotel, una pensión, el mercado
The bank, the post office, a telephone	El banco, correos, un teléfono
The north, south, east, west	El norte, sur, este, oeste
The mountains, the sea, the country	La montaña, el mar, el campo
The beach, the valley	La playa, el valle

MY CAR, DRIVING

Can you tell me where the gas station is?

Fill up, please

My car is broken

Where is the nearest car factory?

The clutch, accelerator, breaks

The blinkers, the steering wheel

Could you check my car for me?

Do I turn to the left, right?

Dangerous cross

CONDUCIR

¿☺Puede, ☺puedes decirme dónde hay una gasolinera?

Lleno, por favor

Mi coche se ha estropeado

¿Dónde está el taller más cercano?

El embrague, el acelerador, los frenos

Los intermitentes, el volante

¿Puede hacer una revisión a mi coche?

¿Giro a la izquierda, derecha?

Cruce peligroso

SPENDING MONEY

How much does it cost...?

Could you give me two postcards?

It's cheap, expensive, very expensive

It's too long, short

It's big, small

It fits me, it doesn't fit me

Where can I find the nearest shop?

Is there a supermarket in the area?

DE COMPRAS

¿Cuánto cuesta...?

¿☺Me da, ☺me das dos postales?

Es barato, caro, muy caro

Es demasiado largo, corto

Es grande, pequeño

Me queda bien, me vale, no me vale

¿Dónde puedo encontrar la tienda más cercana?

¿Hay algún supermercado en la zona?

SHOULD I TAKE MY UMBRELLA?   EL TIEMPO

What will the weather be like today?

It's cold, hot

It's warm, it is freezing

It's raining

I am cold, I am hot

Is the weather going to change?

¿Qué tiempo va a hacer hoy?

Hace frío, hace calor

Hace bueno, hace muchísimo frío

Está lloviendo

Tengo frío, tengo calor

¿Va a cambiar el tiempo?

WILL I FIND A BED?

Where can I find a pension?

Is there a good hostel in the village?

I would like an accommodation

A light bedroom, please

Bed and breakfast

Single bed, two beds, queen bed

Please, could you give me the key?

Is there any place to camp?

I would like a bathroom in the room

Is there hot water?

ALOJAMIENTO

¿Dónde podría encontrar una pensión?

¿Hay algún hotel bueno en el pueblo?

Quisiera alojamiento

Una habitación con luz, por favor

Cama y desayuno

Una cama, dos camas, cama de matrimonio

¿Por favor, me puede dar la llave?

¿Hay algún camping?

Quisiera una habitación con baño

¿Hay agua caliente?

S.O.S. HELP

Where is it the nearest hospital?

We need a doctor

I need help!

Watch out!

I have a big problem

Be careful

AYUDA

¿Dónde está el hospital más cercano?

Necesitamos un doctor

¡Necesito ayuda!

¡Cuidado!

Tengo un gran problema

Ten cuidado

MISSING HOME

I would like to send a telegram

I would like to make a phone call

A collect call, please

Did I receive any message?

CONTACTO

Quisiera mandar un telegrama

Quisiera llamar por teléfono

LLamada a cobro revertido

¿He recibido algún mensaje?

PERSONAL QUESTIONS

Are you on vacation?

Do you live here?

What do you do?

I am a lawyer, a teacher

I am student, a nurse, journalist

PREGUNTAS PERSONALES

¿☺Está usted,☺estás de vacaciones?,

¿☺Vive usted aquí , ☺vives aquí?

¿ A qué ☺se dedica, ☺te dedicas?

Soy abogado, profesor

Soy estudiante, enfermera, periodista

Are you married?	¿☺Está usted casado, ☺estás casado?
How many children do you have?	¿☺Cuántos hijos tiene, ☺ tienes?
How old are you?	¿☺Cuántos años tiene, ☺cuántos años tienes?
Do you have brothers or sisters?	¿☺Tiene ,☺tienes hermanos?
Would you like to go out for a drink?	¿☺Le gustaría, ☺te gustaría salir a tomar algo?

CARDINAL NUMBERS

Zero, one,two, three, four, five, six, seven, eight, nine, ten

Cero,-un,uno,una-,dos, tres,cuatro, cinco, seis,siete,ocho,nueve,diez

eleven, twelve, thirteen, fourteen, fifteen, sixteen, seventeen, eighteen, nineteen

once, doce, trece, catorce, quince, dieciséis, diecisiete, dieciocho, diecinueve

twenty, thirty, forty, fifty, sixty,seventy, eighty, ninety, a hundred

veinte, treinta, cuarenta, cincuenta, sesenta, setenta, ochenta, noventa, cien

two hundred,three hundred, four hundred, five hundred... a thousand

doscientos, trescientos, cuatrocientos, quinientos, seiscientos, setecientos, ochocientos, novecientos, mil

ORDINAL NUMBERS

First, second, third, fourth, fifth, sixth, seventh, eighth, ninth,tenth

Primero, segundo, tercero, cuarto, quinto, sexto, séptimo, octavo, noveno, décimo

HOURS

O'clock

Half past

Quarter to

Quarter past

Ten to five

Twenty past five

QUE HORA ES

En punto (Son las cinco en punto/ son las cinco)

Y media (Son las cinco y media)

Menos cuarto (Son las cinco menos cuarto)

Y cuarto (Son las cinco y cuarto)

Las cinco menos diez

Las cinco y diez

MEASURES	**POCO A POCO**
A little bit	Un poco, un poquito
A lot	Mucho
Not much	No mucho

Learn Spanish Online

http://www.123teachme.com/learn_spanish/exercises_basic_spanish_all

http://webtech.kennesaw.edu/jcheek3/spanish.htm

http://www.davidreilly.com/spanish/

http://www.studyspanish.com/

http://www.studyspanish.com/freesite.htm

http://spanish.speak7.com/

http://www.rosettastone.com/learn-spanish

Words You Might Need

hinga a tu madre (fu*k your mom)

cabron/a (sort of like saying dumbass)

pendejo/a (about the same as cabron but more vulgar)

puto/a (gay for a man, sl*t for a woman)

joto (sort of like the equivalent of *****t; for men only)

tortillera (literally tortilla-maker; a lesbian)

mierda (sh*t)

come mierda (eat sh*t)

vete a la chingada (go to hell)

no se te para (you can't get a bon*r)

coger (to f*ck but in other countries it means to grab)

ojete (sort of like calling someone a douchebag)

Top Three Curse Words

1) Qué Cabrón! (kehh cabrON)

In reality, 'cabrón' refers to a big male goat, with giant horns. As the old Spanish saying goes, a man whose wife is cheating on him is called a 'cabrón' i.e. his horns are growing. So everyone started using 'Que Cabrón!'(What a bastard!), to swear at others. It's quite a mild cuss, and often used just as a sarcastic remark instead of a real curse.

2) Hijo de puta (e-hho-deh-PU-tah)

Translated to the English swear word, 'son of a bitch!' It's used in the exact same way as English, except ten times the frequency. It is however mostly used to tease someone, especially as a sarcastic or envious remarks. Your friend gets a promotion – hijo de puta! Your brother is travelling around the world- hijo de puta! He just bought a 40inch plasma TV- hijo de puta!

3) Los cojones! (los co-hho-nehs)

The Spanish men are known as 'Machotes' (macho men who are proud of their balls), and so, besides the toros (bulls) and the corridas(running of the bulls), they love to show their masculinity by adding the word 'Cojones' (literally means 'testicals') to their colorful language. It tends to be used more like the word 'Bullshit!' in English, in occasions when someone is trying to give you some crappy excuse, you would respond with 'Los Cojones!'

Chapter
ten
Shipping Your Car to
Colombia from Panama

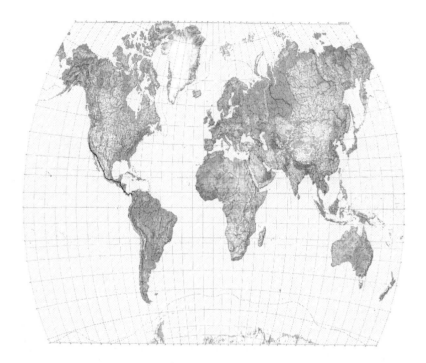

It's a big world out there, go see it.

"Music in the soul can be heard by the universe."
- Lao Tzu

Shipping to Colombia is fairly easy. You need is money, patience and paperwork—Spanish is always helpful. You will need a Carnet de Passages et Dounes, if you don't have one then things will be difficult once you get to South America.

Reportedly, you may ship your vehicle to ship to Cartagena and Buenaventura. This article is based on shipping a container to Cartagena, Columbia. Cartagena is a privately run port and has security and thus is the better option of the two.

Find a shipping company

Upon trying to find a shipping company in Colon we were told that we could easily get a ride but that we'd have to leave the vehicle behind. We looked for a freight boat leaving Coco Solo, an incredibly ass-backwards place with some dubious characters always looking at us with seemingly unpleasant intentions. Check it out is you are on foot but with a vehicle you'll have to go elsewhere.

In Colon there is the Cristobal Port near the bus station. There are many shipping agents scattered throughout the myriad of buildings and banking establishments. Ask around, the going price is around $1000—we found one for $750 but it didn't include a container, not recommended unless you don't mind risking the interior of the vehicle and all its contents. At the entrance to the port is the office of Seaboard Marine and we found they could do it for $950, they seemed the most knowledgeable and trustworthy.

For your $950 you get the following:-

$700—20 foot container, big enough for a large SUV
$75—place vehicle in the container, strap it down and seal it
$150—load the container onto the ship
$25—paperwork (only pertaining to the shipping, not customs etc)

Note that this covers all costs at the Panama side. Once it arrives in Colombia there is more to pay, as usual.

We had to go and arrange the shipping reservation at their offices in Panama City. They're on Via Espana, on the 12 floor of a tower block called Plaza Regency. The Bill of Lading was soon drawn up and the vehicle was booked on a ship called Curacao, sailing the following Thursday. We could either pay in Panama City or in Colon. We'd recommend paying in PC, there is an ATM at the bottom of the Regency Tower block.

For the **Bill of Lading** (BOL) they need a consignee address which is your address in Colombia. We didn't have any hotel in mind so we just picked a hotel from our guide. For the shippers address residential home addresses is suitable. Make sure the BOL specifies pier-to-pier shipping and not 'door-to-door'. Also ensure the BOL states that the car is used.

Customs

Once the shipping is sorted it was up to us to do the customs side of things. This is all done on the outskirts of Panama City and is easy. However, we mistakenly thought that we could do this in Colon so we had to use an agent the day before shipping which cost us $35. She was good though and worth it if you can't be bothered to do it yourself but it's no different to a land border paper chase and easy if you know how—always best to use the local talent for this sort of thing.

First go to the office of the Policia Tecnica Judicial (PTJ) with the car. A guy looks at the vehicle document and checks the chassis number against that of the vehicle. They also check in their files that the vehicle isn't stolen. You get a document, valid for 8 days, which certifies that all is correct. This costs nothing and is fairly quick.

Next step is the customs, which is about a mile away. When we entered Panama they asked us by which border we'd be leaving the country and for which destination. Obviously we said we'd be leaving by sea for Colombia. This is written on the document 'Control de Vehiculos' you get at the border and aids the paperwork at customs when leaving the country. Here you get a document called 'Permiso 130' and the vehicle is stamped out of the owners passport. This costs $8 and is also straightforward.

At the docks

One of the benefits of using Seaboard is that their Colon offices are right beside the customs offices at the Cristobal port entrance. All the people working there know each other and we soon had the usual cursory vehicle inspection and all our papers stamped before driving into the maze of containers to find our little empty one waiting for us with a couple of port workers ready to help out. We took off the roof racks and put it on the so the vehicle could fit into the container. Then it was tied down, the seal put in place and its number and the container number noted down. We left the port with just a bag of clothes each and got the bus back to Panama City for $2. Taxis to the airport, 20kms outside the city at Tocumen, cost about $20 so we got the bus which dropped us off at the entrance for 25 cents each!

Getting to Colombia

Unfortunately it wasn't possible for us to go on the ship with the vehicle so we had to fly. It was actually cheaper to fly via Bogota with Avianca instead of going direct to Cartagena with Copa airlines. We used this to have an afternoon and night in Bogota to see what it was like. It was wicked. Flight cost $158 one-way.

Getting the Landy out

Arriving in Cartagena we phoned the Seaboard office there and they confirmed the ship would arrive the following day and we arranged to meet at the office. We arrived and the Seaboard people ascertained which port the container was in and printed us off the original BOL. They also wrote a letter to the Socieadad Portuario (the Cartagena port authorities) to say that the container is only pier to pier and not door to door shipping which was wrongly specified on the BOL.

Port

Go to the ground floor of the port offices at the Socieadad Portuario and fill in a form to get registered on their database (you get a 'NIT' number). Then you will be given 2 bills to pay pertaining to unloading the container and having it opened. One was for 170,000 pesos and the other for 193,000 pesos, about $150 dollars. Customs cost nothing. There is a cirrus (not visa) cash machine in the office and two bank windows to pay at where they accept Colombian cash only. Once the bills are paid they give you a white piece of paper which says which warehouse the container will be at. Next go upstairs and see Hernando Tovar who is very helpful and arranges a time for unloading the container. It's best to arrange this for the next morning if possible.

Customs

Next go to the DIAN offices which are a five minute walk down the main road and around the corner. Give them the Carnet which they photocopy along with your passport. Try and arrange for a customs inspector to be there at the time the container is opened. They should talk to Hernando at the port and arrange things but it didn't work out for us. You really don't need to pay the 'tramites' guys, who wait around outside the offices, $60 to do this part for you.

Opening the container

Get a magnetic security pass from the downstairs port office (have to swap ID for it, try and use some other ID, not passport as you will need it later) and enter the port area through the revolving gate. Go to the warehouse office where they give you a paper with the authorization to leave the port with your vehicle. One of the guys dressed in blue will open the container. While waiting you can watch the teams of police who search almost everything which is being exported very thoroughly. Once the container is opened you have to drive the car to a secure car park full of expensive new cars and wait for the customs guy to turn up.

When the customs guy arrives (we had to go and get him from the DIAN offices) he checks the chassis number against the Carnet, has a quick look in the back and then signs the Carnet, tears off his piece and writes the car details into your passport (no stamp for it). That's it as far as customs is concerned but getting the car out of the port involves a bit more hassle.
Getting out of the port.

Go back to the warehouse and ask for someone to release the goods. If no one will do it go and see Hernando and he'll sort it. The authorization paper gets stamped and you have to sign it and put your fingerprint on it too.

That's it. Drive out into the streets of Cartagena and point your GPS south.

Drive Me Loco!

The End

WITHDRAWN

Made in the USA
Charleston, SC
12 June 2014